THE
ULTIMATE
BABY
BOOMER
TRIVIA BOOK

Exploring TV, Cinema, Sport, Science, Music and More from the 50s and 60s

By

Jonathan Redwood

Contents

THE FIFTIES

The 1950s in the United States, a decade marked by post-war prosperity and burgeoning consumerism, offers a fascinating glimpse into the cost of living during a time of economic growth and societal change. As the nation emerged from World War II, the average yearly income rose substantially from $3,210 in 1950 to $5,010 in 1959, reflecting a period of financial well-being for many Americans.

Housing was a cornerstone of the American dream in the 1950s, with the median home price starting at $7,354 in 1950 and climbing to $11,900 by 1960. These homes, often in burgeoning suburbs, were symbols of stability and success for the average family. The advent of panelized construction and drywall in home building enabled the rise of "cookie cutter" tract housing, shaping the modern suburb.

The 1950s also saw a significant shift in consumer goods, influenced heavily by television and advertising. Color television, a luxury item, had the RCA Victor CT 100 priced at $1,000 in 1954, later reduced to $495. Black and white television sets, more common, were available around $100. Various household appliances were also popular, including items like the Sunbeam 12W automatic mixer at $46.95 and Kenmore automatic toaster for $12.95, indicative of the era's push-button convenience in kitchens.

Automobiles were another symbol of status and practical necessity for suburban living. The average price for a new car was $1,510 at the start of the decade, reaching $2,200 by the end. However, these cars often required more maintenance and had shorter lifespans compared to modern vehicles.

Groceries and everyday items reflected the economic conditions of the time. Basic items like bread cost around 18-19 cents per loaf, while a pound of sirloin steak was priced at 77 cents in 1950. Consumer electronics, another growing market, included items like the Toshiba 6TP-314 transistor radio at $39.95 and Kodak Pony II camera for $33.

The 1950s set the stage for American consumerism, with spending habits established during this decade continuing to influence modern lifestyles.

Despite the changes in specific products and technology, the patterns of spending on homes, cars, and consumer goods remain a significant part of American life.

TELEVISION (PROGRAMS AND TV SERIES) - 25 trivia

The Golden Age of Television - 1950s TV Programs and Series

In the 1950s, American society experienced a monumental shift with the advent of television, marking the dawn of what is now celebrated as the Golden Age of Television. This transformative period saw the humble television set evolve from a luxurious novelty to a quintessential fixture in living rooms across the nation, altering the landscape of entertainment and daily life in the United States.

As television became more accessible, it introduced a new era of storytelling and entertainment, profoundly impacting American culture. The era was characterized by an array of shows that catered to diverse tastes and interests, from comedy and drama to westerns and variety shows, each leaving an indelible mark on the fabric of American society.

The living rooms of America buzzed with the laughter and drama brought forth by iconic shows such as "I Love Lucy," where Lucille Ball's comedic genius shone brightly, and "The Honeymooners," which showcased Jackie Gleason's unforgettable portrayal of Ralph Kramden. These shows were more than mere entertainment; they were a reflection of the era's societal norms and aspirations.

Variety shows like "The Ed Sullivan Show" and "The Milton Berle Show" became synonymous with family entertainment, introducing Americans to a myriad of acts and performances. Meanwhile, dramas such as "Perry Mason" and "Gunsmoke" captivated audiences with gripping storylines and complex characters. The 1950s also saw the rise of groundbreaking shows like "The Twilight Zone," created by Rod Serling, which pushed the boundaries of television storytelling.

The era was rich with characters who became household names, transcending the screen to become part of American folklore. Figures like Desi Arnaz's Ricky Ricardo in "I Love Lucy," Sid Caesar in "Your Show of Shows," and the beloved canine hero Lassie captured the hearts of viewers. Even less remembered but equally impactful characters from shows like "Our Miss Brooks," featuring the talented Eve Arden, and "The Life and Legend of Wyatt Earp," starring Hugh O'Brian, played a significant role in shaping the television landscape of the 1950s.

The influence of television extended beyond entertainment, becoming a mirror to the societal changes and aspirations of the time. It was a medium that brought families together, sparked conversations, and created a shared experience that united the nation.

As we delve into the engaging quizzes at the end of this chapter, we journey back to this enchanting era of television. These quizzes are designed not just to test your knowledge but also to rekindle memories of the diverse programs, characters, and stars of the 1950s - a time when television was not just a pastime but a vital part of American life. So, let us immerse ourselves in the nostalgia of the Golden Age of Television and revisit an era that reshaped entertainment and society.

1. What was Lucille Ball known for in the 1950s?

A) Hosting a game show

✓ B) Starring in "I Love Lucy"

C) A dramatic role in "Perry Mason"

D) Being a news anchor

E) Hosting a talk show

2. Desi Arnaz played which character in "I Love Lucy"?

✓ A) Ricky Ricardo

B) Fred Mertz

C) Himself

D) Ethel Mertz

E) Don Ricardo

3. What was Milton Berle's popular nickname due to his television success?

A) Mr. Television

✓ B) The King of Comedy

C) The TV Maestro

D) The Showman

E) The Great Entertainer

4. On which TV show did Sid Caesar primarily perform?

✓ A) The Sid Caesar Show

B) Your Show of Shows

C) Caesar's Hour

D) The Comedy Hour

E) Saturday Night Live

5. Jackie Gleason is famous for his role in which 1950s TV series?

✓ A) The Honeymooners

B) The Jackie Gleason Show

C) The Life of Riley

D) I Love Lucy

E) The Ed Sullivan Show

6. Bob Hope was best known in the 1950s for?

A) His film career

B) Hosting "The Bob Hope Show"

C) His role in "I Love Lucy"

✓ D) Stand-up comedy

E) Being a game show host

7. Rod Serling was the creator of which influential TV series?

A) The Twilight Zone

B) Alfred Hitchcock Presents

C) The Outer Limits

D) Night Gallery

E) Star Trek

8. Ed Sullivan is best remembered for hosting:

A) The Ed Sullivan Show

B) Sullivan's Travels

C) The Tonight Show

D) The Merv Sullivan Show

E) This is Your Life

9. Red Skelton was famous for:

A) His dramatic roles in films

B) Hosting a news program

C) His variety show

D) Being a game show host

E) Writing sitcoms

10.   Art Carney is best known for his role as:

A) Ralph Kramden in "The Honeymooners"

✓ B) Norton in "The Honeymooners"

C) Himself in "The Art Carney Show"

D) A detective in "Dragnet"

E) A comedian in "The Red Skelton Show"

11.   Audrey Meadows starred in which TV series?

A) I Love Lucy

B) The Honeymooners

C) The Twilight Zone

✓ D) Gunsmoke

E) Perry Mason

12.   Dinah Shore was best known in the 1950s for her:

A) Acting in sitcoms

✓ B) Variety show

C) Role in a drama series

D) News broadcasting

E) Game show hosting

13.   Perry Como was a:

A) Movie actor

✓ B) Variety show host

C) Sitcom star

D) News anchor

E) Game show host

14.   George Burns and Gracie Allen starred together in:

A) The George Burns Show

B) The Gracie Allen Show

✓ C) The George Burns and Gracie Allen Show

D) Burns and Allen at the Movies

E) The Comedy Hour

The Poodle Skirt

The poodle skirt remains one of the most recognizable symbols of 1950s fashion, embodying the era's playful spirit and youthful rebellion. Originating in the United States, the skirt was a circle skirt, a simple and wide design that fell just below the knee. Its most distinctive feature was the appliqué of a poodle, often accompanied by a sequined leash that spiraled up to the waistband. Created by designer Juli Lynne Charlot in 1947, the poodle skirt quickly rose to popularity among teenage girls. It became synonymous with the decade's youth culture, partly thanks to its feature in popular media and its association with the rock 'n' roll dance scene. The skirt's wide hem was perfect for the period's popular dance moves, twirling gracefully to the music of Elvis Presley and Chuck Berry. Beyond its aesthetic appeal, the poodle skirt also represented a shift towards more casual, fun-loving attire, breaking away from the more restrictive fashion norms of previous decades. This whimsical garment was more than just a fashion statement; it was an emblem of post-war optimism and the burgeoning independence of young women in mid-century America.

_____

15. Jack Benny was famous for his:

A) Role in westerns

✓ B) Variety show

C) News reporting

D) Talk show

E) Game show appearances

16. Who played Superman in "Adventures of Superman" (1952-1958)?

A) Kirk Alyn

✓ B) George Reeves

C) Christopher Reeve

D) Dean Cain

E) Tom Welling

17. What was the profession of the title character in "Cheyenne" (1955-1963)?

A) Sheriff

B) Cowboy

C) Soldier

D) Doctor

E) Lawyer

18. In "The George Burns and Gracie Allen Show" (1950-1958), what was the relation between the two main characters?

A) Brother and Sister

✓ B) Husband and Wife

C) Neighbors

D) Business Partners

E) Friends

19. On "The Roy Rogers Show" (1951-1957), what was the name of Roy Rogers' horse?

A) Trigger

✓ B) Silver

C) Scout

D) Champion

E) Bullet

20. Who played the title role in "The Donna Reed Show" (1958-1966)?

A) Donna Douglas

✓ B) Donna Reed

C) Mary Tyler Moore

D) Barbara Billingsley

E) Elizabeth Montgomery

21. "Our Miss Brooks" (1952-1956) was centered around a character who was a:

A) High School Teacher

B) Nurse

C) Secretary

D) Journalist

E) Police Officer

22. Who portrayed Wyatt Earp in "The Life and Legend of Wyatt Earp" (1955-1961)?

A) Hugh O'Brian

B) James Garner

C) Steve McQueen

D) Clint Eastwood

E) John Wayne

23.   What was the setting of "The Life and Legend of Wyatt Earp"?

A) Dodge City, Kansas

B) Tombstone, Arizona

C) San Francisco, California

D) Deadwood, South Dakota

E) Abilene, Texas

24.   In "The Roy Rogers Show," who was Roy Rogers' female co-star?

A) Dale Evans

B) Annie Oakley

C) June Carter

D) Mary Tyler Moore

E) Barbara Stanwyck

25.   "Our Miss Brooks" was unique for its time due to its focus on:

A) Science fiction themes

B) A strong, independent female lead

C) Musical numbers

D) Animated sequences

E) Espionage and mystery

Crucipuzzle N. 1

Hidden words: what are the actor's names of the protagonists of the series I love Lucy?

```
D B G B L U F O N D A C W
E E U E B B O N A N Z A H
C R N A E I Z L U L S B A
E L S V N A Z L C O M O T
M E M E N L I Z M L H A S
B N O R Y S E A O D A D M
E S K A E A N D Y R R G Y
R E E D L C A E S A R R L
B R W E L L E S D G I O I
R L A S S I E E S N E U N
I I U I B U R N S E T C E
D N A C B E N N E T T H R
E G N A Y A R T H U R O Z
```

Allen: Creator and first host of "The Tonight Show," known for his comedy and music.

Amos: One of the characters from the groundbreaking radio and TV show "Amos 'n' Andy."

Andy: Another key character from "Amos 'n' Andy," known for humorous situations.

Arthur: Actress known for her stage and TV work, later starred in "The Golden Girls."

Beaver: The young lead character of the TV show "Leave It to Beaver."

Bennett: Famous for his music career, also appeared on television in the 1950s.

Benny: Jack Benny, a renowned comedian and actor known for "The Jack Benny Program."

Berle: Known as "Mr. Television," hosted the popular "Texaco Star Theater."

Bonanza: One of the longest-running Western TV series in the U.S.

Burns: Comedian and actor, known for "The George Burns and Gracie Allen Show."

Caesar: Comedian and actor, known for his work on "Your Show of Shows."

Como: Perry Como, a popular singer and television host known for "The Perry Como Show.

December Bride: A sitcom centered around the adventures of a middle-aged widow.

Desilu: Production company founded by Desi Arnaz and

Lucille Ball.

Dragnet: Pioneering police drama series known for its realistic depiction of police work.

Fonda: Celebrated actor who appeared in live television plays during the 1950s.

Groucho: Host of the comedy quiz show "You Bet Your Life."

Gunsmoke: Long-running TV Western about a marshal in Dodge City.

Harriet: From "The Adventures of Ozzie and Harriet," portraying the family's matriarch.

Lassie: The titular character of a long-running TV series about a heroic collie.

Lucy: The beloved character portrayed by Lucille Ball in "I Love Lucy."

Ozzie: From "The Adventures of Ozzie and Harriet," based on the real-life Nelson family.

Reed: Actress known for her lead role in "The Donna Reed Show."

Serling: Creator and host of the iconic anthology series "The Twilight Zone."

Welles: Acclaimed filmmaker and actor, known for his innovative work in film and TV.

What's My Line?: A popular panel game show where celebrities guessed the occupations of guests.

Zorro: The masked vigilante character from the TV series "Zorro."

CINEMA - 15 trivia

The Golden Era of Hollywood - 1950s Cinema

Welcome to the dazzling world of 1950s cinema, an era where Hollywood reached new heights in movie production and storytelling. This was a decade marked by the clash of color and black-and-white, the grandeur of epic filmmaking, and the emergence of new stars who would become legends. The 1950s stood at the crossroads of traditional cinema and the birth of modern filmmaking, a time when movies were not just entertainment but a reflection of society's aspirations and fears.

In this era, Hollywood was much more than a place; it was a dream factory. Iconic studios like MGM, Warner Bros., and Paramount were at their peak, churning out films that ranged from gripping dramas to enchanting musicals. This was the age of Technicolor, bringing a vividness to the screen that mirrored the optimism of post-war America.

The decade saw the rise of directors who became auteurs, leaving indelible marks on cinema history. Names like Alfred Hitchcock, Billy Wilder, and Elia Kazan were not just behind the camera; they were crafting new visual languages and narratives. Their films - from "Rear Window" to "On the Waterfront" - were more than stories; they were windows into the human psyche.

And who can forget the stars who lit up the screen? The 1950s introduced us to the raw intensity of Marlon Brando, the captivating charm of Audrey Hepburn, and the ethereal grace of Grace Kelly. Actors like James Dean and Marilyn Monroe didn't just play characters; they became icons of an era, symbols of rebellion and glamour.

The Quizzes: A Journey Through 1950s Cinema

As we embark on our cinematic journey with the upcoming quizzes, prepare to be transported back to the golden era of Hollywood. You'll encounter questions about some of the most influential films, directors, and stars of the 1950s. From the sweeping romance of "Roman Holiday" to the gritty realism of "A Streetcar Named Desire," these quizzes cover the breadth of this transformative era.

Test your knowledge on the masterpieces that defined a generation - the epic storytelling of "Ben-Hur," the innovative techniques of "Singin' in the Rain," and the dramatic intensity of "Rebel Without a Cause." Dive into the lives and works of the era's most celebrated actors and directors, and rediscover the films that continue to inspire and captivate audiences today.

So, grab your popcorn and settle in for a nostalgic trip down memory lane. It's time to revisit the allure and magic of 1950s Hollywood - an era that shaped not only the film industry but also left a lasting imprint on global culture. Lights, camera, action!

1. Who directed "Rear Window" (1954)?

A) Alfred Hitchcock

B) Orson Welles

C) Billy Wilder

D) Stanley Kubrick

E) John Ford

2. Which actor played the lead role in "Rebel Without a Cause" (1955)?

A) Marlon Brando

B) James Dean

C) Paul Newman

D) Montgomery Clift

E) Gregory Peck

3. Who was the leading actress in "Roman Holiday" (1953)?

A) Audrey Hepburn

B) Grace Kelly

C) Elizabeth Taylor

D) Ingrid Bergman

E) Katharine Hepburn

4.   Which movie features the famous song "Singin' in the Rain"?

A) An American in Paris

B) High Noon

C) Singin' in the Rain

D) The Band Wagon

E) On the Town

5.   In "The African Queen" (1951), who played the role of Charlie Allnut?

A) Humphrey Bogart

B) Clark Gable

C) Cary Grant

D) John Wayne

E) Spencer Tracy

6.   "A Streetcar Named Desire" (1951) featured which actress as Blanche DuBois?

A) Vivien Leigh

B) Bette Davis

C) Marilyn Monroe

D) Elizabeth Taylor

E) Grace Kelly

7.   Who played the lead in "Sunset Boulevard" (1950)?

A) Gloria Swanson

B) Greta Garbo

C) Marlene Dietrich

D) Joan Crawford

E) Bette Davis

8.   "The Seven Year Itch" (1955) is famous for a scene featuring Marilyn Monroe standing over a subway grate. What was her character's name?

A) Elsie Marina

B) Lorelei Lee

C) Sugar Kane

D) The Girl

E) Rose Loomis

9.   In "The Bridge on the River Kwai" (1957), who played the role of Colonel Nicholson?

A) William Holden

B) Alec Guinness

C) Jack Hawkins

D) Sessue Hayakawa

E) Charles Laughton

10.   "Some Like It Hot" (1959) was directed by:

A) Billy Wilder

B) Alfred Hitchcock

C) Welles

D) John Huston

E) Frank Capra

11.   "On the Waterfront" (1954) features which actor as Terry Malloy?

A) Marlon Brando

B) James Dean

C) Paul Newman

D) Kirk Douglas

E) Burt Lancaster

12.   In "Shane" (1953), who played the title character?

A) Alan Ladd

B) John Wayne

C) Gary Cooper

D) Gregory Peck

E) Clint Eastwood

13. Who was the director of "The Ten Commandments" (1956)?

A) Cecil B. DeMille

B) William Wyler

C) John Ford

D) Alfred Hitchcock

E) David Lean

14. In "Vertigo" (1958), who played the role of Madeleine Elster/Judy Barton?

A) Grace Kelly

B) Kim Novak

C) Ingrid Bergman

D) Janet Leigh

E) Eva Marie Saint

15. "East of Eden" (1955) marked the first major role for which actor?

A) Paul Newman

B) James Dean

C) Marlon Brando

D) Montgomery Clift

E) Steve McQueen

Singin' in the Rain

One of the most beloved films of the 1950s, "Singin' in the Rain," starring Gene Kelly, Debbie Reynolds, and Donald O'Connor, is renowned for its memorable musical numbers and vibrant choreography. A lesser-known fact about this classic is the challenging circumstances under which the iconic title song "Singin' in the Rain" was filmed. Gene Kelly performed the famous scene where he dances through the streets in the pouring rain while battling a high fever of 103 degrees Fahrenheit. Despite his illness, Kelly delivered an energetic and flawless performance, splashing through puddles with an infectious joy that has captivated audiences for generations. The rain in the scene was mixed with milk to ensure it showed up on camera, adding another layer of complexity to the filming process. This scene, now legendary in the annals of cinema, is a testament to Kelly's dedication and professionalism, forever defining the spirit of the golden age of Hollywood musicals.

Crucipuzzle N. 2

Hidden words: A famous 1953 film directed by Howard Hawks and starring Marylin Monroe.

B	E	N	H	U	R	G	I	A	N	T	H	D
G	O	D	Z	I	L	L	A	G	E	G	N	A
W	N	G	T	A	Y	L	O	R	I	A	H	V
I	C	H	A	P	L	I	N	E	M	L	I	I
L	O	D	T	R	E	L	L	W	O	L	T	S
D	O	E	E	M	T	C	E	S	N	A	C	E
E	P	R	N	A	S	N	K	K	R	B	H	C
R	E	K	E	E	N	W	P	A	O	O	C	L
R	R	E	L	B	A	E	F	Z	E	U	O	I
E	R	L	B	H	E	G	R	A	N	T	C	F
L	E	L	G	A	R	L	A	N	D	E	K	T
W	A	Y	N	E	O	G	I	G	I	V	N	D
S	U	N	S	E	T	B	L	V	D	E	E	S

All About Eve: A critically acclaimed film known for its sharp dialogue and exploration of theater life.

Ben-Hur: Epic historical drama known for its grand scale and chariot race scene.

Bogart: Humphrey Bogart, iconic actor known for his roles in film noir and dramas.

Chaplin: Charlie Chaplin, legendary actor and filmmaker, continued to influence cinema in this decade.

Clift: Montgomery Clift, actor known for his intense performances and method acting.

Cooper: Gary Cooper, actor known for his performances in Westerns and dramas.

Davis: Bette Davis, actress known for her strong and often unsympathetic characters.

Dean: James Dean, an actor who became a cultural icon of teenage disillusionment.

Garland: Judy Garland, actress and singer known for her emotional performances.

Giant: A film known for its portrayal of Texas culture and its epic scope.

Gigi: A musical film known for its lavish production and memorable score.

Godzilla: A Japanese film that became an international sensation, spawning a long-lasting franchise.

Grant: Cary Grant, actor known for his charm and roles in romantic comedies and thrillers.

Hawks: Howard Hawks, a director known for his versatility and numerous classic films.

Hitchcock: Alfred Hitchcock, director known for his mastery of suspense and psychological thrillers.

Kazan: Elia Kazan, director known for his influential and often controversial films.

Kelly: Grace Kelly, actress known for her beauty and performances in Hitchcock films.

Leigh: Vivien Leigh, actress known for her dramatic performances and intense roles.

Monroe: Marilyn Monroe, actress and sex symbol known for her roles in comedies and dramas.

Newman: Paul Newman, actor known for his charismatic performances and blue eyes.

Peck: Gregory Peck, actor known for his commanding presence and roles as moral figures.

Rebel: "Rebel Without a Cause," a film known for its portrayal of teenage angst.

Sunset Blvd: A film known for its critique of Hollywood and memorable opening scene.

Taylor: Elizabeth Taylor, actress known for her beauty and roles in dramatic films.

Wayne: John Wayne, actor known for his roles in Westerns and as an American icon.

Welles: Orson Welles, actor and director known for his innovative work in film.

Wilder: Billy Wilder, director known for his sharp wit and successful films across genres.

SPORT - 25 trivia

The Athletic Titans of the 1950s – A Golden Era in Sports

Step into the vibrant world of 1950s sports, an era where athleticism and competition reached exhilarating new heights. In this golden age, sports were not just games: they were epic battles that defined heroes and inspired nations. The 1950s witnessed a surge in the popularity of various sports, with baseball, boxing, and basketball leading the charge, capturing the hearts of fans and creating icons whose legacies endure to this day.

Baseball reigned supreme, hailed as America's favorite pastime. The decade saw legendary figures like Joe DiMaggio, Mickey Mantle, and Jackie Robinson, who not only dazzled on the field but also broke barriers and set new standards. Robinson, in particular, became a symbol of courage and change as he shattered the color barrier in Major League Baseball.

In the boxing ring, titans like Rocky Marciano and Sugar Ray Robinson thrilled spectators with their prowess, power, and poise. Marciano's unblemished record and Robinson's silky skills in the ring made them more than champions; they were the very epitome of boxing greatness.

The hardwood courts of basketball witnessed the rise of stars like Bill Russell and Bob Cousy, athletes who revolutionized the game with their skill and strategic play. Their contributions helped elevate basketball from a mere sport to a national spectacle.

Meanwhile, in tennis, players like Althea Gibson and Pancho Gonzales captivated audiences with their groundbreaking talent and fierce determination. Gibson, in particular, broke racial and gender barriers, becoming an icon of resilience and excellence.

Upcoming Quizzes: Test Your Knowledge of Sports Legends

As you dive into the quizzes that follow, prepare to embark on a journey through the 1950s, a time when sports figures were not just athletes but legends who transcended their respective games. These quizzes will challenge your knowledge and celebrate the achievements of some of the most iconic sports figures of the decade.

You'll encounter questions about the titans of the baseball diamond, the kings of the boxing ring, the wizards of the basketball court, and the pioneers of the tennis world. Each question is an opportunity to relive the glory days of these athletes and to appreciate the impact they had not only on sports but on society as a whole.

So, get ready to step back in time and experience the thrill, the drama, and the triumphs of the 1950s sports era. Whether you're a sports aficionado or just curious about this pivotal era in sports history, these quizzes offer a fun and engaging way to connect with the legends who shaped the world of athletics. Let the games begin!

1. Which team did Joe DiMaggio play for during his entire MLB career?

A) New York Yankees

B) Boston Red Sox

C) Chicago Cubs

D) Los Angeles Dodgers

E) St. Louis Cardinals.

2. Jackie Robinson broke the Major League Baseball color barrier with which team?

A) Brooklyn Dodgers

B) New York Yankees

C) Boston Red Sox

D) Chicago Cubs

E) Philadelphia Phillies

3. Mickey Mantle was known for playing which position predominantly for the New York Yankees?

A) Pitcher

B) First Baseman

C) Outfielder

D) Catcher

E) Shortstop

4.   Willie Mays is best known for playing with which MLB team in the 1950s?

A) San Francisco Giants

B) New York Giants

C) Chicago Cubs

D) Milwaukee Braves

E) Brooklyn Dodgers

5.   Yogi Berra, a legendary baseball figure, was a part of which team in the 1950s?

A) New York Yankees

B) Boston Red Sox

C) Brooklyn Dodgers

D) Chicago White Sox

E) Detroit Tigers

6.   Which MLB team was Ted Williams associated with during his career?

A) Boston Red Sox

B) Baltimore Orioles

C) New York Yankees

D) Detroit Tigers

E) Chicago White Sox

7. Hank Aaron began his major league career with which team?

A) Milwaukee Braves

B) Atlanta Braves

C) New York Yankees

D) Chicago Cubs

E) Los Angeles Dodgers

8. Stan Musial spent his entire MLB career with which team?

A) St. Louis Cardinals

B) Cincinnati Reds

C) Philadelphia Phillies

D) Pittsburgh Pirates

E) Chicago Cubs

9. Warren Spahn is best known for his time as a pitcher with which MLB team?

A) Milwaukee Braves

B) New York Yankees

C) Boston Red Sox

D) Chicago Cubs

E) Philadelphia Phillies

10. Bob Feller spent his entire career with which MLB team?

A) Cleveland Indians

B) Chicago White Sox

C) Kansas City Royals

D) Detroit Tigers

E) Minnesota Twins

11. Which professional boxer was known as "Sugar"?

A) Sugar Ray Robinson

B) Floyd Patterson

C) Rocky Marciano

D) Archie Moore

E) Carmen Basilio

12. Rocky Marciano was a champion in which weight class?

A) Middleweight

B) Welterweight

C) Lightweight

D) Heavyweight

E) Featherweight

13. Floyd Patterson became the youngest heavyweight champion in 1956 at what age?

A) 21

B) 22

C) 23

D) 24

E) 25

14. Archie Moore held the light heavyweight world championship for how many consecutive years?

A) 5 years

B) 9 years

C) 11 years

D) 7 years

E) 13 years

15. Carmen Basilio was famous for winning championships in which boxing weight class?

A) Middleweight

B) Welterweight

C) Lightweight

D) Heavyweight

E) Featherweight

The Milan Miracle

The 1950s in American sports is often remembered for its baseball heroes, but one of the most remarkable events took place in college basketball. The 1954 NCAA Basketball Championship featured a David vs. Goliath story when the relatively unknown team from Milan High School in Indiana, with a student body of just 161, won the state championship. Their victory was against the odds, as they faced much larger and more established schools. The championship game, where Milan defeated Muncie Central with a last-second shot, has become an iconic moment in the history of American high school sports. This game, often referred to as the "Milan Miracle," later inspired the movie "Hoosiers," capturing the essence of underdog triumph and the magic of basketball in small-town America. This event remains a symbol of hope and determination, showcasing that with teamwork and perseverance, even the smallest team can achieve the unimaginable.

---

16. Bill Russell is famously associated with which NBA team?

A) Boston Celtics

B) Los Angeles Lakers

C) Philadelphia 76ers

D) New York Knicks

E) Chicago Bulls

17. Wilt Chamberlain, a dominant figure in the NBA, began his career with which team?

A) Philadelphia/San Francisco Warriors

B) Los Angeles Lakers

C) Boston Celtics

D) Milwaukee Bucks

E) Chicago Bulls

18. Elgin Baylor was a star player for which NBA team in the late 1950s?

A) Boston Celtics

B) Minneapolis/Los Angeles Lakers

C) Philadelphia 76ers

D) New York Knicks

E) Detroit Pistons

19. Which NFL player was known as "The Golden Arm"?

A) Johnny Unitas

B) Otto Graham

C) Joe Perry

D) Jim Brown

E) Y.A. Tittle

20. Maurice Richard played for which NHL team during his entire career?

A) Montreal Canadiens

B) Detroit Red Wings

C) Toronto Maple Leafs

D) Chicago Blackhawks

E) Boston Bruins

21. What milestone did Althea Gibson achieve in tennis?

A) First African American to win Wimbledon

B) Won a Calendar Year Grand Slam

C) Youngest player to win the US Open

D) Longest winning streak in tennis history

E) Most Grand Slam titles in the 1950s

22. Bob Mathias was known for his achievements in which sport?

A) Boxing

B) Baseball

C) Football

D) Decathlon

E) Basketball

23.   Which baseball player was known as "The Commerce Comet"?

A) Mickey Mantle

B) Hank Aaron

C) Willie Mays

D) Ted Williams

E) Stan Musial

24.   Pancho Gonzales was a leading figure in which sport during the 1950s?

A) Tennis

B) Golf

C) Boxing

D) Basketball

E) Baseball

25.   Who was the heavyweight boxing champion undefeated throughout the 1950s?

A) Rocky Marciano

B) Floyd Patterson

C) Sugar Ray Robinson

D) Archie Moore

E) Carmen Basilio

Crucipuzzle N. 3

Hidden words: Which two New York Yankees stars of the 1950s, one a renowned slugger and the other a famed catcher, both became Baseball Hall of Famers?

H	K	A	L	I	N	E	C	O	U	S	Y	T
O	U	S	P	A	H	N	M	I	N	C	G	I
G	P	L	A	Y	E	R	K	E	I	H	R	T
A	Y	M	L	A	Y	N	E	N	T	E	A	T
N	M	B	A	S	I	L	I	O	A	I	H	L
A	B	O	W	X	N	Z	P	M	S	N	A	E
A	A	A	O	E	I	E	L	N	T	S	M	L
R	Y	E	E	R	S	M	A	Y	S	O	A	N
O	L	W	A	D	E	T	N	D	B	H	Y	S
N	O	O	M	I	K	I	T	A	R	N	G	T
H	R	M	I	D	D	L	E	C	O	F	F	A
B	E	L	I	V	E	A	U	I	W	B	E	R
W	I	L	L	I	A	M	S	R	N	R	A	R

Aaron: Braves' right fielder who later broke Babe Ruth's home run record.

Arizin: Philadelphia Warriors basketball star, known for his scoring ability.

Basilio: Middleweight boxing champion, known for bouts with Sugar Ray Robinson.

Baylor: Minneapolis Lakers star, known for his rebounding and scoring prowess.

Beliveau: Montreal Canadiens center, known for his skill and sportsmanship in hockey.

Brown: Cleveland Browns fullback, known for his power running.

Cousy: Boston Celtics point guard, famous for his ball-handling and playmaking.

Graham: Cleveland Browns quarterback, known for his leadership and passing.

Heinsohn: Boston Celtics forward, known for his scoring and rebounding.

Hogan: Professional golfer, famous for his ball-striking ability and major wins.

Howe: Detroit Red Wings right winger, known for his scoring and longevity.

Hull: Chicago Blackhawks left winger, known for his fast skating and scoring.

Kaline: Detroit Tigers outfielder, known for his hitting and fielding prowess.

Layne: Detroit Lions quarterback, known for his passing and leadership.

Maxim: Light heavyweight boxer, known for his durability and technical skills.

Middlecoff: Professional golfer, known for his precision and major championship wins.

Mikita: Chicago Blackhawks center, known for his skillful play and scoring ability.

Moore: Light heavyweight champion boxer, known for his longevity in the sport.

Mays: New York Giants outfielder, known for his all-around baseball talent.

Player: South African golfer, known for his success in major championships.

Plante: Montreal Canadiens goaltender, innovator of the goalie mask in hockey.

Snead: Professional golfer, known for his smooth swing and PGA Tour victories.

Spahn: Milwaukee Braves left-handed pitcher, known for his dominance and longevity.

Starr: Green Bay Packers quarterback, known for his poise and leadership.

Tittle: Quarterback known for his time with the San Francisco 49ers and New York Giants.

Unitas: Legendary quarterback for the Baltimore Colts, known for his game-winning drives.

West: Los Angeles Lakers guard, known for his scoring and clutch play.

Williams: Boston Red Sox left fielder, known for his hitting prowess and last .400 season.

LITERATURE & ART - 30 trivia

The Pinnacle of Creativity - Art, Literature, and Architecture in the 1950s

Welcome to the fascinating world of the 1950s, an era that witnessed a blossoming of creativity across art, literature, and architecture. This was a decade that embraced both the traditional and the avant-garde, shaping a legacy that continues to captivate us. As we turn the pages back to this vibrant era, we discover a tapestry woven with the genius of influential artists, novelists, and architects whose work not only reflected but also shaped the culture of their time.

In the realm of literature, the 1950s saw a proliferation of voices that challenged and enchanted. Authors like J.D. Salinger and Vladimir Nabokov captured the complexities of human experience in their groundbreaking novels, "The Catcher in the Rye" and "Lolita." Meanwhile, in the world of art, figures like Jackson Pollock and Andy Warhol were redefining the boundaries of artistic expression. Pollock's drip paintings became synonymous with Abstract Expressionism, while Warhol's pop art played with the ideas of consumerism and celebrity.

The 1950s were also a golden age for architecture, with visionaries like Frank Lloyd Wright and Le Corbusier shaping the skylines and the very way we live. Wright's organic architecture, showcased in masterpieces like Fallingwater, blurred the lines between the built and natural environments. Le Corbusier's modernist designs reimagined urban living, offering a vision of a future that was both functional and beautiful.

Upcoming Quizzes: Exploring the Icons of the 1950s

As we delve into the upcoming quizzes, prepare to embark on a journey through the artistic, literary, and architectural wonders of the 1950s. These quizzes will challenge you to explore the works and lives of the decade's most influential figures. From the captivating stories penned by master novelists to the revolutionary art that changed the way we see the world, and the architectural marvels that redefined our spaces, each question offers a window into the creative spirit of the 1950s.

So, get ready to immerse yourself in the creativity and innovation that defined this remarkable era. Whether you're an art enthusiast, a literary aficionado, or an admirer of groundbreaking architecture, these quizzes promise to offer insights and surprises, celebrating the enduring legacy of the 1950s' most influential creators. Let's step back in time and rediscover the magic of this pivotal decade in art, literature, and architecture.

1. In "Lord of the Flies" by William Golding, who is the leader of the choirboys?

A) Ralph

B) Jack

C) Simon

D) Piggy

E) Roger

2. What kind of animal is Charlotte in "Charlotte's Web" by E.B. White?

A) Pig

B) Horse

C) Spider

D) Sheep

E) Dog

3. In "Lolita" by Vladimir Nabokov, who is the narrator obsessed with?

A) Charlotte Haze

B) Dolores "Lolita" Haze

C) Annabel Leigh

D) Valeria

E) Mona Dahl

4. "Night" by Elie Wiesel is set during which historical event?

A) World War I

B) The Cold War

C) World War II

D) The Vietnam War

E) The Korean War

5. In "The Chronicles of Narnia" by C.S. Lewis, what is the name of the lion who is a central character?

A) Reepicheep

B) Mr. Tumnus

C) Edmund

D) Aslan

E) Eustace

6. In "Flowers for Algernon" by Daniel Keyes, what type of being is Algernon?

A) Human

B) Mouse

C) Dog

D) Computer

E) Alien

7. What is the setting of "The Martian Chronicles" by Ray Bradbury?

A) An alternate Earth

B) The Moon

C) Mars

D) Venus

E) Jupiter

8. Who tries to stop Christmas from coming in "How the Grinch Stole Christmas!" by Dr. Seuss?

A) The Cat in the Hat

B) The Lorax

C) The Grinch

D) Horton

E) Sam-I-Am

9. "The Crucible" by Arthur Miller is about which historical event?

A) The American Civil War

B) The Salem Witch Trials

C) The Boston Tea Party

D) The First Thanksgiving

E) The California Gold Rush

10.   What is the main theme of "Things Fall Apart" by Chinua Achebe?

A) The clash between different cultures

B) Time travel

C) Space exploration

D) A detective story

E) A love story

11.   Who is the main character in "The Once and Future King" by T.H. White?

A) Sir Lancelot

B) King Arthur

C) Merlin

D) Guinevere

E) Mordred

12.   In "Waiting for Godot" by Samuel Beckett, what are the two main characters doing?

A) Waiting for someone named Godot

B) Running a marathon

C) Searching for a treasure

D) Fighting a war

E) Going on a journey

13.   What is the primary setting of "The Haunting of Hill House" by Shirley Jackson?

A) A hotel

B) A castle

C) A hill house

D) A school

E) A hospital

14.   In "The Voyage of the Dawn Treader" by C.S. Lewis, who is the king of Narnia?

A) Peter

B) Edmund

C) Caspian

D) Aslan

E) Eustace

_____

The Lost Music of the Soviet Union (50)

In the 1950s, amidst the stringent censorship in the Soviet Union, a unique form of music distribution emerged, known as 'Bone Music' or 'Ribs'. Western music, which was often banned by the authorities, found its way into the hands of Soviet youth through an underground and ingenious method. Enterprising individuals began using discarded X-ray films, often sourced from hospitals, to create makeshift records. These X-ray sheets were repurposed to etch bootleg copies of prohibited Western music, from jazz to rock 'n' roll. The sound quality of these 'Bone Records' was far from perfect, but they became a symbol of rebellion and a window to the outside world for many Soviet citizens. This clandestine practice not only highlighted the ingenuity in overcoming censorship but also underscored the insatiable hunger for cultural freedom during a time of heavy political repression.

_____

15.   What is the primary focus of "Foundation" by Isaac Asimov?

A) The fall of an empire

B) A detective mystery

C) A love story

D) Time travel

E) A war between planets

16.   "A Separate Peace" by John Knowles is set during which time period?

A) The Roaring Twenties

B) World War II

C) The Civil War

D) The Great Depression

E) The Renaissance

17.   In "The Magician's Nephew" by C.S. Lewis, what is the Wood between the Worlds?

A) A forest

B) A city

C) A series of magical portals

D) A school

E) An ocean

18.   Mark Rothko is known for his distinctive style in painting. What is a key characteristic of his work?

A) Geometric shapes

B) Detailed portraits

C) Large blocks of color

D) Landscape scenes

E) Political imagery

19.   Willem de Kooning's works are categorized under which art movement?

A) Cubism

B) Abstract Expressionism

C) Surrealism

D) Pop Art

E) Dadaism

20.   Andy Warhol's most iconic work is arguably his series of paintings depicting what?

A) Celebrities

B) Everyday consumer goods

C) Political figures

D) Landscapes

E) Historical events

21.   Norman Rockwell is best known for his illustrations for which magazine?

A) Time

B) Vogue

C) The New Yorker

D) The Saturday Evening Post

E) National Geographic

22.   Georgia O'Keeffe is especially celebrated for her paintings of what?

A) Urban landscapes

B) Abstract shapes

C) Flowers and natural forms

D) Sea creatures

E) Futuristic cities

23.   Robert   Rauschenberg   is   known   for   his "Combines," which are:

A) Only paintings

B) Only sculptures

C) Mixed media artworks

D) Digital art pieces

E) Photography series

24.   Jasper Johns' work often features which common motif?

A) Fruit bowls

B) Automobiles

C) Flags

D) Animals

E) Faces

25.   Roy Lichtenstein was a leading figure in which art movement?

A) Impressionism

B) Abstract Expressionism

C) Cubism

D) Pop Art

E) Surrealism

26. What distinguishes Andy Warhol's Marilyn Monroe series?

A) Black and white photography

B) Use of neon colors

C) Monochromatic blue shades

D) Silkscreen prints

E) Oil on canvas

27. Georgia O'Keeffe is particularly associated with which American region in her paintings?

A) The Northeast

B) The Midwest

C) The South

D) The Southwest

E) The Pacific Northwest

28. Frank Lloyd Wright is known for designing which iconic house, a prime example of his "organic architecture" philosophy?

A) The Rietveld Schröder House

B) Villa Savoye

C) Fallingwater

D) The Guggenheim Museum

E) Farnsworth House

29.   Le Corbusier was a pioneer in which architectural style?

A) Gothic Revival

B) Baroque

C) Modernism

D) Art Deco

E) Brutalism

30.   Ansel Adams is most famous for his photographs of which national park?

A) Yellowstone National Park

B) Yosemite National Park

C) Grand Canyon National Park

D) Zion National Park

E) Rocky Mountain National Park

Title: Rosalind Franklin: The Shadowed Scientist of DNA

In the scientific revolution of the 1950s, Rosalind Franklin was a key yet often overlooked figure in the discovery of DNA's structure. Born in 1920 in London, Franklin excelled as a chemist and X-ray crystallographer, specializing in X-ray diffraction techniques.

Her most notable work was Photo 51, an X-ray diffraction image of DNA that provided crucial clues about its double helix structure. However, the recognition of her contribution was overshadowed by scientists James Watson, Francis Crick, and Maurice Wilkins, who received the Nobel Prize in 1962 for discovering the structure of DNA, partly based on Franklin's research.

Rosalind Franklin died young, at just 37, from ovarian cancer, likely related to her exposure to radiation during her work. Despite her early death, her contribution to science remains invaluable, and in subsequent years, her role in the discovery of DNA's structure has been finally recognized and celebrated.

_____

Crucipuzzle N. 4

Hidden words: He won the Nobel Prize for Literature in 1954.

```
F L A N N E R Y J O N E S
E E F R A N K U P D I K E
R R N E V K E R O U A C G
L E S L E M I L L E R L I
I B A L D W I N K T L S N
N M E I O H E C M I R O S
G A V S N K E R T E S Z B
H I A O I B Y S B L H W E
E L N N N K N L E T N A R
T E S I R H A V A G W R G
T R E O O B E L L O W H A
I T G J T N P Y N C H O N
S M I T H L E W I T T L Y
```

Albers: Josef Albers, abstract painter and color theorist.

known for his "Homage to the Square" series.

Avedon: Richard Avedon, influential fashion and portrait photographer.

Baldwin: James Baldwin, notable for his essays on race and his novel "Go Tell It on the Mountain."

Bellow: Saul Bellow, a leading novelist and short story writer, known for "The Adventures of Augie March."

Ellison: Ralph Ellison, known for his novel "Invisible Man," a pivotal book on African-American life.

Evans: Walker Evans, photographer known for documenting American life during the Great Depression.

Ferlinghetti: Lawrence Ferlinghetti, poet, painter, and co-founder of City Lights Booksellers & Publishers.

Flannery: Flannery O'Connor, writer known for her Southern Gothic style and short stories.

Frank: Robert Frank, photographer known for his book "The Americans," capturing post-war American life.

Ginsberg: Allen Ginsberg, poet, a leading figure in the Beat Generation, known for his poem "Howl."

Gorky: Arshile Gorky, painter who had a significant influence on Abstract Expressionism.

Johns: Jasper Johns, painter and sculptor known for his works featuring flags, numbers, and maps.

Jones: James Jones, known for his novel "From Here to Eternity."

Kertész: André Kertész, photographer known for his contributions to photographic composition and photojournalism.

Kerouac: Jack Kerouac, a central figure of the Beat Generation, known for "On the Road."

LeWitt: Sol LeWitt, an artist linked to the Conceptual art and Minimalist movements.

Mailer: Norman Mailer, writer and journalist known for "The Naked and the Dead."

Miller: Arthur Miller, playwright known for "The Crucible" and "Death of a Salesman."

Nevelson: Louise Nevelson, known for her monochromatic, wooden wall pieces and outdoor sculptures.

Plath: Sylvia Plath, poet and author, known for her confessional poetry and the novel "The Bell Jar."

Pynchon: Thomas Pynchon, author known for his dense and complex novels.

Roth: Philip Roth, author known for his self-referential and controversial writing style.

Smith: David Smith, an American sculptor known for his pioneering work in abstract metal sculptures, often using welded steel.

Steinbeck: John Steinbeck, author of "East of Eden" and "The Grapes of Wrath."

Still: Clyfford Still, painter and one of the leading figures of Abstract Expressionism.

Updike: John Updike, writer known for his Rabbit series.

Warhol: Andy Warhol, a leading figure in the visual art movement known as Pop Art.

CARTOONS & COMICS - 20 trivia

A Nostalgic Journey Through 1950s Comics and Cartoons

Step into the vibrant and imaginative world of the 1950s – a decade where comics and cartoons were not just mere entertainment but a cultural phenomenon that captured the hearts of millions. This was an era when storytelling leaped from the pages and screens, bringing laughter, adventure, and a touch of whimsy into the everyday life of post-war America.

In this golden era, comics such as "Little Archie," "Sugar and Spike," and "Li'l Jinx" became staples in every child's reading list, weaving stories that were both relatable and enchantingly surreal. The antics of "Pat the Brat" and "Melvin the Monster" offered humor with a dash of mischievous charm, while "The Brain" and "Little Ike" showcased the lighter side of childhood curiosity and ingenuity.

The world of animation, too, was in its renaissance. "The Heckle and Jeckle Show" and "Mighty Mouse" brought a unique blend of humor and heroism to the small screen. The adventures of "Yogi Bear" and "Huckleberry Hound" broke new grounds in animation, setting a high bar for character-driven storytelling. nd who could forget the fast-paced chases of "The Road Runner Show" or the witty escapades in "The Bullwinkle Show"? These cartoons were not just for kids but a delightful escape for adults as well.

Upcoming Quizzes: Exploring the Magic of 1950s Comics and Cartoons

As we embark on the quizzes ahead, get ready to be whisked back to the colorful and charismatic world of 1950s comics and cartoons. These quizzes are designed to rekindle your memories and challenge your knowledge of this enchanting era's most beloved characters and stories.

Whether you're revisiting your childhood favorites or discovering them for the first time, these quizzes will offer a delightful exploration of the creativity and charm that defined the comics and cartoons of the 1950s. Prepare to laugh, reminisce, and maybe even learn a thing or two about this pivotal era in comic and animation history.

So, let's turn back the clock and dive into a world where every page and every frame brimmed with imagination and joy. Welcome to the delightful, humorous, and ever-surprising world of 1950s comics and cartoons!

1."The Brain," a comic series that began in 1956, was known for featuring:

A) A super-intelligent dog

B) A boy with telekinetic powers

C) A genius child with advanced gadgets

D) A robot with human emotions

E) An ordinary child with extraordinary intelligence

2. "Pat the Brat," first published in 1955, was a comic about a:

A) Superhero

B) Mischievous child

C) Talking animal

D) Space adventurer

E) Ghost

3. What was the primary theme of the "Li'l Jinx" comic series, first appearing in 1956?

A) High school drama

B) Everyday life of a young girl

C) Fantasy adventures

D) Time travel

E) Detective stories

4. "Little Archie," first published in 1956, was a spin-off of which popular comic series?

A) Superman

B) Batman

C) Archie Comics

D) Peanuts

E) The Fantastic Four

5. "Melvin the Monster," first appearing in 1956, was known for its:

A) Dark and scary themes

B) Humorous and child-friendly content

C) Educational science stories

D) Action-packed superhero plots

E) Mystery and detective scenarios

6. "Sugar and Spike," created by Sheldon Mayer in 1956, featured stories about:

A) Teenage superheroes

B) Two babies and their adventures

C) Talking animals in a forest

D) Space exploration

E) A time-traveling scientist

7. "Little Angel," first published in 1954, was unique for its portrayal of:

A) An angel living among humans

B) A child detective

C) A young superhero

D) A talking animal

E) A child living in a fantasy world

8. "Super Brat," first appearing in 1954, was notable for its focus on a:

A) Spoiled child with superpowers

B) Brave child in a fantasy realm

C) Young genius and his inventions

D) Child exploring the universe

E) Young detective solving mysteries

9. What was the main theme of "Li'l Tomboy," which debuted in 1956?

A) A girl's adventures in space

B) A tomboyish girl and her daily life

C) A magical fairy in a forest

D) A girl detective solving cases

E) A princess in a medieval kingdom

10. "Little Ike", first published in 1953, was a comic about:

A) A young inventor

B) A baby's imaginative adventures

C) A child prodigy musician

D) A kid detective

E) A miniature superhero

11. "The Heckle and Jeckle Show" featured two main characters who were:

A) Bears

B) Rabbits

C) Dogs

D) Mice

E) Magpies

12. "The Yogi Bear Show" was a spin-off from which other cartoon?

A) The Flintstones

B) The Huckleberry Hound Show

C) Looney Tunes

D) The Jetsons

E) Tom and Jerry

13. What is Mighty Mouse's signature ability in "Mighty Mouse"?

A) Super strength

B) Invisibility

C) Super speed

D) Time travel

E) Shapeshifting

14. "Pixie and Dixie and Mr. Jinks" centers around the conflict between two mice, Pixie and Dixie, and a cat named:

A) Sylvester

B) Tom

C) Felix

D) Garfield

E) Mr. Jinks

15. In "The Huckleberry Hound Show," what type of animal is Huckleberry Hound?

A) A cat

B) A dog

C) A bear

D) A mouse

E) A rabbit

16. "The Road Runner Show" primarily features the chase between which two characters?

A) Tom and Jerry

B) Sylvester and Tweety

C) Yogi Bear and Boo-Boo

D) Road Runner and Wile E. Coyote

E) Fred Flintstone and Barney Rubble

17. What was the main theme of "The Ruff and Reddy Show"?

A) Time travel adventures

B) Space exploration

C) Underwater expeditions

D) Detective mysteries

E) Magical world exploration

18. "The Bullwinkle Show" featured a moose named Bullwinkle and his friend, who is a:

A) Dog

B) Squirrel

C) Rabbit

D) Cat

E) Bird

19. Mr. Magoo, the character from "Mr. Magoo," is known for his:

A) Super strength

B) Magical powers

C) Near-sightedness

D) Super speed

E) Ability to fly

20. "Felix The Cat" is known for his:

A) Magic bag of tricks

B) Detective skills

C) Ability to talk to animals

D) Time machine

E) Super speed

Crucipuzzle N. 5

Hidden Words: Which obscure and poorly animated American TV show from the 1950s, featuring a pelican protagonist, has gained a cult following for its notably low production quality?

```
T  T  R  H  T  A  R  Z  A  N  E  A  O
W  D  O  N  A  L  D  D  U  C  K  T  N
E  D  A  I  R  O  N  M  A  N  U  A  D
E  V  D  P  O  P  E  Y  E  L  M  A  C
T  E  R  N  C  T  U  R  P  K  E  B  I
Y  A  U  B  A  E  S  O  W  H  G  L  N
F  R  N  E  S  T  D  A  G  W  O  O  D
P  C  N  T  P  I  H  U  S  A  O  N  E
D  H  E  T  E  N  J  D  N  Y  F  D  R
T  I  R  Y  R  T  H  E  O  T  Y  I  E
V  E  R  O  N  I  C  A  O  H  P  E  L
B  A  T  M  A  N  E  L  P  O  I  C  L
P  E  T  E  R  P  A  N  Y  R  A  N  A
```

Archie: Red-haired teenager from the "Archie Comics" series, set in the fictional town of Riverdale.

Batman: DC Comics superhero, a vigilante of Gotham City known for his bat-themed costume and gadgets.

Betty: Character from "Archie Comics," known for her girl-next-door charm and rivalry with Veronica over Archie.

Blondie: Title character of the comic strip "Blondie," known for her family life and iconic sandwiches.

Casper: Friendly ghost character known for his kind-hearted nature in comics and animated films.

Cinderella: Classic Disney princess known for her rags-to-riches story and glass slippers.

Dagwood: Character from the comic strip "Blondie," known for his love of large sandwiches and comical mishaps.

Donald Duck: Disney character known for his short temper and distinctive voice.

Goofy: Disney character known for his clumsiness and good-natured goofiness.

Hawkman: DC Comics character known for his wings and ancient weaponry.

Iron Man: Marvel Comics superhero, a wealthy industrialist who wears a suit of armor with advanced technology.

Jughead: Character from "Archie Comics," known for his laid-back attitude and insatiable appetite.

Peter Pan: Disney character known for never growing up and his adventures in Neverland.

Pluto: Disney character, Mickey Mouse's loyal pet dog.

Popeye: Sailor character known for gaining superhuman strength after eating spinach.

Road Runner: Warner Bros. cartoon character known for his incredible speed and "Beep, Beep" sound.

Snoopy: Charles Schulz's "Peanuts" comic strip character, Charlie Brown's imaginative and loyal dog.

Tarzan: Jungle hero known for his adventures in the wild and his call of the wild.

Thor: Marvel Comics superhero, the Norse god of thunder wielding a magical hammer.

Tintin: A young, adventurous reporter from the Belgian comic series "The Adventures of Tintin," created by Hergé, known for his global escapades and distinctive quiff

Tweety: Warner Bros. cartoon character, a cute yellow bird often targeted by Sylvester.

Veronica: Character from "Archie Comics," known for her wealthy lifestyle and rivalry with Betty over Archie.

SCIENCE - 10 trivia

Chapter Introduction: The Dawn of a New Era - Science and Technology in the 1950s

Welcome to the exhilarating and transformative world of the 1950s, a decade that marked the dawn of a new era in science and technology. This was a time of unparalleled innovation and discovery, a period where boundaries were pushed, and the impossible was made possible. The 1950s laid the foundations for technological advancements that would shape the future and change the lives of millions in the United States and beyond.

Imagine a world on the brink of the digital age. The 1950s saw the birth of the computer revolution with the creation of the UNIVAC I, the first commercially successful computer, which opened new horizons in data processing and business operations. The development of the integrated circuit, the forerunner to the microchip, set the stage for the miniaturization of electronic devices, paving the way for the computers and smartphones we use today.

This decade was also a time of great strides in space exploration and science. The launch of Explorer 1, America's first satellite, marked the nation's entry into the space race, igniting dreams of reaching the stars. In biology, the discovery of the double helix structure of DNA by Watson and Crick revolutionized our understanding of genetics and heredity.

In everyday life, the introduction of inventions like the modem and the credit card began to reshape how people communicated and conducted transactions, signaling the start of a new digital and consumer age.

Upcoming Quizzes: A Journey Through the Science and Technology of the 1950s

As we embark on the quizzes that lie ahead, prepare to be transported back to an era of groundbreaking discoveries and inventions. These quizzes will take you on a fascinating journey through the scientific achievements and technological wonders of the 1950s.

From the first steps into outer space to the genesis of the digital world, each question will offer a glimpse into the innovations that shaped the modern landscape. Whether you're a science enthusiast, a technology buff, or just curious about how far we've come, these quizzes promise an engaging exploration of a decade that redefined the boundaries of possibility.

So, let's dive into the spirit of the 1950s – an era of curiosity, ambition, and forward-thinking – and discover how science and technology began to weave the fabric of the future. Get ready for a captivating journey into a time when the future was now!

1.In 1953, Francis Crick and James Watson made a groundbreaking discovery in molecular biology. What was it?

A) The structure of proteins

B) The double helix structure of DNA

C) The mechanism of viral infection

D) The process of photosynthesis

E) The formula for nuclear fission

2. The first successful demonstration of a functioning laser, a pivotal moment in optics and photonics, was completed in the 1950s by whom?

A) Gordon Gould

B) Theodore Maiman

C) Charles Townes

D) Arthur Schawlow

E) Albert Einstein

3. Which of the following medical breakthroughs occurred in the 1950s and significantly impacted public health worldwide?

A) Introduction of the first antibiotic

B) Development of the polio vaccine by Jonas Salk

C) Discovery of insulin

D) Invention of the MRI machine

E) Creation of the first artificial heart

4. The invention of the integrated circuit, which laid the foundation for modern electronics, was accomplished by whom in the 1950s?

A) John Bardeen and Walter Brattain

B) William Shockley

C) Jack Kilby and Robert Noyce

D) Lee de Forest

E) Hedy Lamarr

5. In the 1950s, which American astronomer made significant contributions to the understanding of the Milky Way's structure?

A) Edwin Hubble

B) Carl Sagan

C) Walter Baade

D) Harlow Shapley

E) Gerard Kuiper

6. What major development in physics was achieved at Brookhaven National Laboratory in 1952?

A) Discovery of the neutron

B) Invention of the cyclotron

C) First nuclear fusion reaction

D) Observation of the muon neutrino

E) Construction of the first particle accelerator

7. In 1957, which American space observatory was the first to detect the Van Allen radiation belt?

A) Hubble Space Telescope

B) Chandra X-ray Observatory

C) Spitzer Space Telescope

D) Explorer 3

E) James Webb Space Telescope

8. What major advancement in organ transplantation was achieved by Joseph Murray in 1954?

A) First successful heart transplant

B) Development of immunosuppressive drugs

C) First successful kidney transplant

D) Invention of the artificial heart

E) First successful liver transplant

9. What was the primary purpose of the first programmable digital computer, UNIVAC I, which was introduced in the 1950s?

A. Weather forecasting

B. Space exploration calculations

C. Business data processing

D. Nuclear simulations

E. Academic research

10. What significant engineering achievement occurred in 1958 concerning satellite technology?

A) Launch of Sputnik 1

B) Invention of the microchip

C) Launch of Explorer 1

D) First transatlantic television transmission via satellite

E) Development of GPS technology

The Birth of the Videotape Recorder

A significant yet often overlooked technological leap of the 1950s was the development of the videotape recorder (VTR). In 1951, Bing Crosby Enterprises demonstrated the first videotape recording using longitudinal recording on tape. However, it was in 1956 that the technology truly took a monumental step forward with the introduction of the Ampex VRX-1000, the first commercially successful videotape recorder.

This innovation revolutionized the television industry by allowing programs to be recorded, edited, and replayed. Before the advent of the VTR, television was predominantly live or broadcasted via kinescope recordings, which involved recording a TV show off a monitor screen onto film. The VTR made it possible to record directly onto tape, offering much higher quality and the ability to easily edit and reproduce content.

The VTR was a marvel in its time, though cumbersome by today's standards, consisting of large reel-to-reel tapes and standing as tall as a person. Despite its size, the invention paved the way for future developments in media technology, such as home video recorders and, eventually, digital recording and streaming technologies. The VTR represents a landmark in media history, a leap into the modern era of television and video production, vastly influencing how media would be consumed and produced in the subsequent decades.

Crucipuzzle N. 6

Hidden Words: The structure of which molecule was discovered by Watson and Crick in 1953?

C	U	R	I	E	Y	U	K	A	W	A	T	W
H	R	P	L	A	N	C	K	Y	D	E	O	O
A	F	I	B	A	R	D	E	E	N	M	W	X
N	E	W	C	Y	B	K	R	R	A	I	N	W
D	R	I	B	K	A	L	O	G	O	S	E	I
R	M	G	S	E	A	B	O	R	G	I	S	E
A	I	N	L	B	U	S	H	C	B	E	L	N
S	T	E	L	L	E	R	N	A	H	Y	U	E
E	C	R	U	T	H	E	R	F	O	R	D	R
K	S	H	A	N	N	O	N	H	L	E	H	I
H	A	H	N	C	L	I	B	B	Y	O	A	C
A	L	V	A	R	E	Z	H	U	B	B	L	E
R	K	I	W	A	L	D	D	B	E	T	H	E

Alvarez: Luis Alvarez, a physicist known for his work on bubble chambers, winning the Nobel Prize in Physics in 1968.

Bardeen: John Bardeen, co-inventor of the transistor and a two-time Nobel laureate in Physics.

Bethe: Hans Bethe, a physicist who won the Nobel Prize in Physics for his work on the theory of nuclear reactions.

Bloch: Felix Bloch, a physicist who made fundamental contributions to the understanding of magnetism, winning the Nobel Prize in Physics.

Bohr: Niels Bohr, a key figure in the development of atomic physics and quantum theory.

Born: Max Born, a physicist and mathematician who made significant contributions to quantum mechanics.

Bush: Vannevar Bush, an engineer and science administrator known for his work on analog computing and his role in the Manhattan Project.

Chandrasekhar: Subrahmanyan Chandrasekhar, astrophysicist known for the Chandrasekhar limit in stellar evolution.

Crick: Francis Crick, a molecular biologist who co-discovered the structure of DNA.

Curie: Marie Curie, known for her pioneering research on radioactivity.

Fermi: Enrico Fermi, a physicist known for his work on nuclear reactions and the first controlled nuclear reaction.

Gamow: George Gamow, astrophysicist who contributed to the Big Bang theory.

Hubble: Edwin Hubble, an astronomer who played a crucial role in establishing the field of extragalactic astronomy.

Hahn: Otto Hahn, a chemist who discovered nuclear fission.

Hoyle: Fred Hoyle, an astronomer who formulated the theory of stellar nucleosynthesis.

Leakey: Louis Leakey, a paleoanthropologist known for his work in human evolutionary development.

Libby: Willard Libby, a chemist who developed radiocarbon dating, winning the Nobel Prize in Chemistry.

Planck: Max Planck, a physicist who is considered the father of quantum theory.

Rabi: Isidor Isaac Rabi, a physicist who won the Nobel Prize for his discovery of nuclear magnetic resonance.

Rutherford: Ernest Rutherford, known as the father of

nuclear physics.

Salk: Jonas Salk, a medical researcher who developed one of the first successful polio vaccines.

Seaborg: Glenn T. Seaborg, a chemist who contributed to the discovery of several elements and the development of the actinide concept.

Shannon: Claude Shannon, a mathematician, electrical engineer, and cryptographer known as "the father of information theory."

Teller: Edward Teller, a theoretical physicist known for his work on the hydrogen bomb.

Townes: Charles Townes, a physicist known for his work on the theory and application of the maser and laser.

Wald: George Wald, a biologist known for his work on the chemistry of vision, winning the Nobel Prize in Physiology or Medicine.

Wigner: Eugene Wigner, a physicist who made significant contributions to the theory of the atomic nucleus and elementary particles.

Wiener: Norbert Wiener, a mathematician known as the father of cybernetics.

Yukawa: Hideki Yukawa, a theoretical physicist and the first Japanese Nobel laureate, known for his prediction of the meson particle.

MUSIC - 25 trivia

The Dawn of a Musical Era – The Music of the 1950s

Welcome to the 1950s, an era where music not only defined a generation but also set the stage for decades of musical innovation to come. In this chapter. we turn back the clock to a time of jukeboxes, vinyl records, and the birth of rock 'n' roll. Here, we'll explore the sounds and rhythms that captured the hearts of audiences and laid the groundwork for the modern music landscape.

The 1950s was a decade marked by the rise of legendary figures whose music still resonates today. It was the era of Elvis Presley, the "King of Rock 'n' Roll," whose electrifying performances and charismatic style forever changed the music industry. Chuck Berry and Little Richard brought an explosive energy to rock music, influencing countless artists to come.

This was also the decade when jazz and blues flourished, with artists like Miles Davis and John Coltrane transforming the genre with their innovative styles. The smooth crooning of Frank Sinatra and Nat King Cole filled the airwaves, providing the soundtrack to a post-war world that was rapidly evolving.

Doo-wop harmonies echoed in the streets, with groups like The Platters and The Drifters defining a new era of vocal music. Meanwhile, the emergence of rhythm and blues laid the foundation for soul and Motown, genres that would dominate in the decades to follow.

As we embark on a series of quizzes exploring the rich tapestry of 1950s music, you'll have the chance to test your knowledge of the iconic songs, artists, and moments that shaped this pivotal era. From the early days of rock 'n' roll to the timeless melodies of the jazz and swing era, each question will transport you back to a time when music was a vibrant and transformative force in society. So, let's roll back the clock, step into the rhythm, and relive the magical musical journey of the 1950s!

1. "Johnny B. Goode," a song that became an anthem for rock 'n' roll, was performed by...

A. Elvis Presley

B. Jerry Lee Lewis

C. Chuck Berry

D. Little Richard

E. Buddy Holly

2. Which artist is known for the hit song "Jailhouse Rock"?

A. Chuck Berry

B. Johnny Cash

C. Elvis Presley

D. Buddy Holly

E. Ray Charles

3. Ray Charles had a big hit in 1959 with which song?

A. "What'd I Say"

B. "I've Got a Woman"

C. "Georgia on My Mind"

D. "Hit the Road Jack"

E. "Unchain My Heart"

4. "Rock Around the Clock" by Bill Haley & His Comets is notable for being...

A. One of the first rock 'n' roll records

B. A country crossover hit

C. An early example of a music video

D. A blues-inspired track

E. A song from a movie soundtrack

5. Who originally sang the rock and roll classic "Tutti Frutti"?

A. Elvis Presley

B. Chuck Berry

C. Little Richard

D. Jerry Lee Lewis

E. Buddy Holly

6. "I Walk the Line" is a famous song by...

A. Elvis Presley

B. Johnny Cash

C. Carl Perkins

D. Roy Orbison

E. Hank Williams

7. Buddy Holly and the Crickets are known for which hit song?

A. "That'll Be the Day"

B. "Peggy Sue"

C. "Maybe Baby"

D. "Oh Boy!"

E. "Everyday"

8. Which song is a major hit by Fats Domino?

A. "Blueberry Hill"

B. "Ain't That a Shame"

C. "I'm Walkin'"

D. "Whole Lotta Loving"

E. "Blue Monday"

9. "Great Balls of Fire" was famously performed by...

A. Elvis Presley

B. Chuck Berry

C. Little Richard

D. Jerry Lee Lewis

E. Buddy Holly

10. Which artist is known for the song "La Bamba"?

A. Ritchie Valens

B. Elvis Presley

C. Buddy Holly

D. Chuck Berry

E. Eddie Cochran

11. "Heartbreak Hotel" was a major hit for which legendary musician?

A. Jerry Lee Lewis

B. Elvis Presley

C. Chuck Berry

D. Little Richard

E. Buddy Holly

12. Which song by Little Richard is known for its high-energy performance and catchy beat?

A. "Long Tall Sally"

B. "Tutti Frutti"

C. "Good Golly Miss Molly"

D. "Lucille"

E. "Rip It Up"

13. "Mack the Knife," a song that became a top hit, was performed by...

A. Frank Sinatra

B. Dean Martin

C. Bobby Darin

D. Nat King Cole

E. Tony Bennett

14. Who was the artist behind the classic country hit "I Walk the Line"?

A. Hank Williams

B. Johnny Cash

C. Willie Nelson

D. Patsy Cline

E. Jim Reeves

15. "Peggy Sue" was a popular song by which influential rock 'n' roll artist?

A. Elvis Presley

B. Jerry Lee Lewis

C. Buddy Holly

D. Ritchie Valens

E. Eddie Cochran

16. Which band released the groundbreaking rock and roll hit "Rock Around the Clock"?

A. Bill Haley & His Comets

B. The Everly Brothers

C. The Platters

D. The Drifters

E. The Coasters

17. "Whole Lotta Shakin' Goin' On" is a famous song by...

A. Chuck Berry

B. Little Richard

C. Elvis Presley

D. Jerry Lee Lewis

E. Carl Perkins

18. "Why Do Fools Fall in Love" was a hit song for which group?

A. The Platters

B. The Drifters

C. Frankie Lymon & The Teenagers

D. The Coasters

E. The Penguins

19. Which artist is famous for the hit "Summertime Blues"?

A. Eddie Cochran

B. Buddy Holly

C. Gene Vincent

D. Ritchie Valens

E. Carl Perkins

20. "Blueberry Hill," a hit song blending R&B and rock 'n' roll, was performed by...

A. Fats Domino

B. Chuck Berry

C. Little Richard

D. Ray Charles

E. Bo Diddley

21. Which group is known for the 1950s hit "Sh-Boom"?

A. The Platters

B. The Drifters

C. The Chords

D. The Coasters

E. The Penguins

22. Who recorded the original version of "Hound Dog" before Elvis Presley's famous cover?

A. Big Mama Thornton

B. Muddy Waters

C. B.B. King

D. Howlin' Wolf

E. Ruth Brown

23. What was the name of Elvis Presley's first single, recorded in 1953 at Sun Studio?

A. Heartbreak Hotel

B. Love Me Tender

C. That's All Right

D. Blue Suede Shoes

E. Hound Dog

24. What was the title of the first album to top the newly established Billboard album chart in 1956?

A. In the Wee Small Hours

B. Songs for Swingin' Lovers!

C. Songs for Lovers

D. This Is Sinatra!

E. Frank Sinatra Sings for Only the Lonely

25. Which 1950s musician was known as "The Father of Exotica" for his tropical-themed music?

A. Les Baxter

B. Martin Denny

C. Arthur Lyman

D. Yma Sumac

E. Robert Drasnin

Crucipuzzle N. 7

Hidden Words: A Jimmy Driftwood song made famous by Johnny Horton in 1959

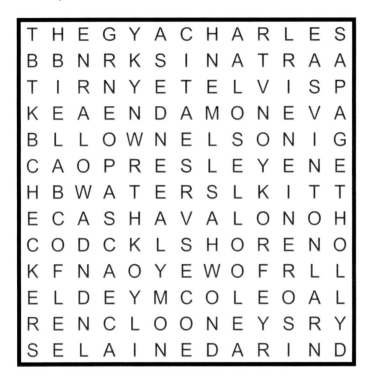

Anka: Paul Anka, a singer-songwriter known for hits like "Diana" and "Put Your Head on My Shoulder."

Avalon: Frankie Avalon, a teen idol known for hits like "Venus" and "Why."

Berry: Chuck Berry, a rock and roll pioneer known for his guitar riffs and hits like "Johnny B. Goode."

Boone: Pat Boone, known for his clean-cut image and hits like "Love Letters in the Sand."

Brewer: Teresa Brewer, a pop and jazz singer known for hits like "Music! Music! Music!"

Cash: Johnny Cash, a country music artist known for his deep voice and hits like "I Walk the Line."

Charles: Ray Charles, a soul music pioneer known for blending rhythm and blues, gospel, and blues.

Checker: Chubby Checker, known for popularizing "The Twist," a dance craze in the early '60s.

Clooney: Rosemary Clooney, a popular singer known for hits like "Come On-a My House."

Cole: Nat King Cole, a singer and jazz pianist known for his smooth voice and hits like "Unforgettable."

Como: Perry Como, a popular American singer and television personality known for his smooth baritone voice and relaxed singing style, with hits like "Catch a Falling Star" and hosting "The Perry Como Show."

Damone: Vic Damone, a traditional pop and big band singer with a smooth vocal style.

Darin: Bobby Darin, known for hits like "Mack the Knife" and his versatile style.

Day: Doris Day, a singer and actress known for her wholesome image and hits like "Que Sera, Sera."

Elvis: Elvis Presley, the "King of Rock and Roll," known for his charismatic stage presence and hits like "Heartbreak Hotel."

Ford: Tennessee Ernie Ford, a country and gospel singer known for hits like "Sixteen Tons."

Haley: Bill Haley, known for his rock and roll band Bill Haley & His Comets and hits like "Rock Around the Clock."

Holly: Buddy Holly, a central figure in mid-1950s rock and roll, known for his distinctive vocal style.

King: B.B. King, a legendary blues guitarist and singer known for his expressive singing and guitar playing, particularly his use of vibrato and the famed guitar, "Lucille."

Kitt: Eartha Kitt, a singer known for her distinctive voice and hits like "Santa Baby."

Laine: Frankie Laine, a singer known for his hits in the '50s, including "Rawhide."

Lee: Peggy Lee, a jazz and pop singer known for her

seductive vocal style.

Lymon: Frankie Lymon, a rock and roll and R&B singer known for "Why Do Fools Fall in Love."

Nelson: Ricky Nelson, a teen idol known for hits like "Hello Mary Lou."

Page: Patti Page, known for her traditional pop music hits like "Tennessee Waltz."

Presley: Elvis Presley, an iconic figure in rock and roll, known for his distinctive voice and style.

Rydell: Bobby Rydell, a teen idol known for hits like "Wild One."

Sedaka: Neil Sedaka, a pop singer known for hits like "Calendar Girl."

Shore: Dinah Shore, a singer and television personality known for her warm singing style.

Sinatra: Frank Sinatra, a legendary singer known for his smooth voice and phrasing.

Vinton: Bobby Vinton, a pop singer known for hits like "Blue Velvet."

Waters: Ethel Waters, a singer and actress known for her blues, jazz, and gospel music.

THE SIXTIES

The 1960s in the United States was a dynamic decade, marked not only by cultural and social changes but also by noticeable shifts in the cost of living. During this era, the average family income rose significantly, reflecting the nation's growing economy.

In terms of housing, the average price of a new home in 1960 was around $11,900, climbing to about $20,600 by 1969. Rent prices followed a similar upward trajectory, with the average monthly rent for a two-bedroom apartment in a metropolitan area rising from approximately $100 in 1960 to around $175 in 1969.

Transportation costs were also notable. In 1960, the average price of a gallon of gas was about $0.31, which slightly increased to around $0.35 by 1969. The cost of a new car in 1960 was around $2,600, and by 1969, this had risen to approximately $3,270.

When it came to consumer goods, the 1960s saw a variety of prices. For instance, a super-powerful juicer was priced at $48.95 in 1964, and an electric can opener could be purchased for $12.97. The iconic transistor radio, a must-have gadget of the decade, saw its price drop over the years, from $5.88 in 1964 to $3.88 by 1969 for a basic model.

Groceries, a daily necessity, also reflected the economic conditions of the time. For example, in 1960, a loaf of bread cost about 19-35 cents, depending on the brand. Meat prices varied, with steak priced between 59 and 89 cents per pound, and turkey at 35 cents per pound in 1967. Everyday items like a 1lb pack of Nabisco Ritz crackers were available for 29 cents.

Education expenses also rose during this period. The average tuition and fees for a private four-year college in 1960 were around $1,400 per year, increasing to about $2,800 by 1969. Public four-year colleges saw a rise from $243 to $484 annually in the same period.

Entertainment costs, including movie tickets, records, and live performances, also increased. A movie ticket in 1960 cost around 69 cents, climbing to about $1.00 by 1969. The price of a new record album went from around $3.98 to $5.98 over the decade.

Clothing prices reflected the changing fashion trends of the 60s. For instance, a men's suit cost around $65 in 1960, increasing to about $89 by 1969. A woman's dress was priced at around $12 in 1960 and rose to approximately $20 by the end of the decade.

The medical field also saw an increase in costs. A general practitioner visit in 1960 cost about $10, which increased to $15 by 1969. The average cost of a hospital stay per day was around $30 in 1960, rising to about $50 by 1969.

TELEVISION (PROGRAMS AND TV SERIES) - 25 trivia

The Swinging Sixties - A Television Revolution

Welcome to the vibrant and transformative era of the 1960s, a decade where television not only mirrored but also shaped the cultural and social revolution. This was the time when television evolved from being a novelty to a staple in American households, a window to a world of diversity, innovation, and change. As we tune into this chapter, we explore how TV programs and series of the 1960s reflected and influenced the customs and zeitgeist of the time.

In the 1960s, television became the medium that captured the essence of an era marked by upheaval and progress. It was a period of bold experimentation in programming, with shows that broke traditional molds and challenged societal norms. Sitcoms like "I Dream of Jeannie" and "Bewitched" brought fantasy and magic into living rooms, while "The Andy Griffith Show" and "The Dick Van Dyke Show" offered slices of American life with a mix of humor and heart.

This decade also saw the rise of thought-provoking dramas and action-packed series. "Star Trek" not only took viewers on interstellar adventures but also tackled complex social issues, making it a symbol of progressive thought. "The Twilight Zone" delved into the realms of science fiction and fantasy, pushing the boundaries of storytelling.

Groundbreaking variety shows like "The Ed Sullivan Show" continued to be a platform for diverse and cutting-edge talent, reflecting the dynamic cultural shifts of the 60s. The decade also witnessed the emergence of soap operas like "Dark Shadows," adding a touch of melodrama and intrigue to daytime TV.

Upcoming Quizzes: Reliving the Golden Age of 60s Television

As we switch channels to the quizzes that follow, prepare to embark on a nostalgic journey through the iconic TV programs and series of the 1960s. These quizzes will test your knowledge and rekindle memories of the shows and characters that became household names.

From the laughter-filled episodes of classic sitcoms to the gripping plots of pioneering dramas, and the memorable moments of variety shows, each question will transport you back to an era where television was at the forefront of cultural change.

Whether you're a fan of the classics, a lover of television history, or simply curious about the shows that defined a decade, these quizzes promise a delightful exploration of the 1960s' television landscape. So grab your remote (or rather, your quiz buzzer, and get ready to relive the magic of an era that revolutionized the world of television. Lights, camera, action – welcome to the swinging sixties of TV!

1. What is the name of Andy Taylor's son in The Andy Griffith Show?

A. Opie

B. Barney

C. Floyd

D. Otis

E. Gomer

2. What is Rob Petrie's job in The Dick Van Dyke Show?

A. Lawyer

B. Doctor

C. Comedy writer

D. Teacher

E. Architect

3. What is Samantha's primary magical gesture in "Bewitched"?

A. Snapping her fingers

B. Waving her wand

C. Blinking her eyes

D. Twitching her nose

E. Clapping her hands

4. Where did the Clampett family move from in "The Beverly Hillbillies"?

A. Texas

B. Kentucky

C. Tennessee

D. Oklahoma

E. West Virginia

5. What is the name of the Cartwrights' ranch in "Bonanza"?

A. Southfork Ranch

B. Ponderosa Ranch

C. Lancer Ranch

D. Big Valley Ranch

E. Mustang Ranch

6. Who created "The Twilight Zone"?

A. Gene Roddenberry

B. Rod Serling

C. Alfred Hitchcock

D. Steven Spielberg

E. Ray Bradbury

7. Who is the chief medical officer on the USS Enterprise in "Star Trek"?

A. Captain Kirk

B. Mr. Spock

C. Dr. McCoy

D. Scotty

E. Chekov

8. Who played the Joker in the 1960s Batman TV series?

A. Jack Nicholson

B. Cesar Romero

C. Heath Ledger

D. Jared Leto

E. Mark Hamill

9. Where did Tony Nelson find Jeannie's bottle in "I Dream of Jeannie"?

A. In a shop

B. On a beach

C. In a cave

D. In space

E. In an antique chest

10. "The Munsters": What kind of creature is Grandpa Munster?

A. Vampire

B. Werewolf

C. Frankenstein's monster

D. Mummy

E. Ghost

Bell Bottom Pants

Bell-bottom pants, characterized by their distinct flare from the knee downward, became a fashion sensation in the 1960s and a symbol of the counterculture movement. Initially adopted by the sailors in the early 19th century for their practicality, bell-bottoms experienced a resurgence among the youth of the 1960s as an emblem of rebellion and a departure from conventional styles. This trend was more than just a fashion statement; it was intertwined with the era's broader cultural shifts, including the peace movement, the rise of psychedelic music, and the growing influence of hippie culture. The pants were often made from denim or colorful fabrics and paired with vibrant patterns, fringes, and embroidery, reflecting the decade's embrace of individualism and self-expression. Icons like Jimi Hendrix and Janis Joplin popularized the style, which became synonymous with the Woodstock generation. Bell-bottoms were not only a hallmark of 1960s fashion but also represented a broader desire for social change and freedom of expression, leaving a lasting imprint on fashion history.

----

11. How many passengers set sail on the S.S. Minnow in "Gilligan's Island"?

A. Five

B. Six

C. Seven

D. Eight

E. Four

12. Which famous band made their U.S. television debut on "The Ed Sullivan Show"?

A. The Beatles

B. The Rolling Stones

C. The Beach Boys

D. The Who

E. Pink Floyd

13. What is Dr. Richard Kimble accused of in "The Fugitive"?

A. Kidnapping

B. Robbery

C. Espionage

D. Murder

E. Arson

14. "Get Smart": What is Agent 86's real name?

A. Harry Hoo

B. Larabee

C. Maxwell Smart

D. Siegfried

E. The Chief

15. "The Avengers": Who is John Steed's most famous female partner?

A. Emma Peel

B. Cathy Gale

C. Tara King

D. Purdey

E. Tracy Bond

16. What is the name of the POW camp in "Hogan's Heroes"?

A. Camp X

B. Stalag 13

C. Stalag 17

D. Alcatraz

E. Colditz Castle

17. What role did Raymond Burr play in "Perry Mason"?

A. Detective

B. Judge

C. Prosecutor

D. Defense lawyer

E. Police chief

18. What is the name of the Addams family's butler?

A. Alfred

B. Lurch

C. Jeeves

D. Benson

E. Geoffrey

19. What was Oliver Wendell Douglas' profession before moving to Hooterville in "Green Acres"?

A. Farmer

B. Lawyer

C. Doctor

D. Teacher

E. Banker

20. "Dragnet": What is Sergeant Joe Friday's badge number?

A. 714

B. 321

C. 90210

D. 456

E. 007

21. What is the name of the robot in "Lost in Space"?

A. HAL 9000

B. B-9

C. R2-D2

D. Data

E. C-3PO

22. In which town do the Flintstones live?

A. Bedrock

B. Rockville

C. Stonehenge

D. Boulder City

E. Pebblesburg

23. Who played Marshal Matt Dillon on "Gunsmoke"?

A. Clint Eastwood

B. James Arness

C. John Wayne

D. Gary Cooper

E. Burt Reynolds

24. What is the name of the leader of the IMF team in "Mission: Impossible"?

A. James Bond

B. Ethan Hunt

C. Jim Phelps

D. Jack Ryan

E. Jason Bourne

25. "The Avengers": Which actor played the role of John Steed?

A. Sean Connery

B. Roger Moore

C. Patrick Macnee

D. David Niven

E. Michael Caine

Crucipuzzle N. 8

Hidden Words: What is the name of the classic American TV sitcom set in the fictional community of Mayberry, depicting the life of a widowed sheriff and his son?

```
C L E A V E R Y C A I N E
A R N A Z T N E W H A R T
R D R A G N E T A D A M S
S O H E E H G O M E Z A N
O O B B V O S P O C K D Y
N A L I A S G L E A S O N
G D R O N S M A R T I F F
I D R O D D E N B E R R Y
K A T H Y G E N I E Y I S
I M H D K B A L L C O W E
R S A M E R T Z U T A T E
K R A V I T Z L M O O R E
B O N A N Z A B A T M A N
```

Adams: Agent 99 from "Get Smart," known for her intelligence and wit in the spy comedy series.

Addams: From "The Addams Family," a series featuring a quirky and macabre family.

Arnaz: Desi Arnaz, a Cuban-American actor, musician, and television producer, best known for his role as Ricky Ricardo on the iconic sitcom "I Love Lucy."

Ball: Lucille Ball, famous for her comedic role in "I Love Lucy" and "The Lucy Show."

Batman: A comic book hero brought to life in the campy 1960s television series.

Benny: Jack Benny, a renowned American comedian, vaudevillian, and actor known for his leading role in "The Jack Benny Program.

Bonanza: A popular American Western television series that aired in the 1960s.

Brady: The surname of the family in "The Brady Bunch," a series about a large blended family.

Caine: From "Kung Fu," a series featuring a Shaolin monk traveling through the American Old West.

Carson: Johnny Carson, long-time and iconic host of "The Tonight Show."

Cleaver: The family surname in "Leave It to Beaver," a series about suburban family life.

Dragnet: A police drama series known for its realistic portrayal of law enforcement and its famous intro line, "Just the facts, ma'am."

Genie: From "I Dream of Jeannie," a series about a genie and her astronaut master.

Gleason: Jackie Gleason, an influential American comedian, actor, and musician, known for his role as Ralph Kramden in the television series "The Honeymooners."

Gomez: The patriarch in "The Addams Family," known for his eccentric and loving nature.

Hoss: A character from "Bonanza," known for his size, strength, and kind-hearted nature.

Kirk: Captain James T. Kirk from "Star Trek," known for his leadership on the starship USS Enterprise.

Kravitz: The nosy neighbor in "Bewitched," often suspicious of Samantha's witchcraft.

Lucy: Lucille Ball's iconic character in "I Love Lucy," known for her comedic talent and antics.

Mertz: The landlords and friends of Lucy and Ricky in "I Love Lucy."

Moore: Mary Tyler Moore, known for her role as Laura Petrie on "The Dick Van Dyke Show."

Newhart: Bob Newhart, known for his dry humor and

starring role in "The Bob Newhart Show."

Petrie: Rob Petrie from "The Dick Van Dyke Show," known for his work as a comedy writer and his family life.

Robin: The sidekick of Batman in the "Batman" TV series, known for his acrobatic skills and "Holy" catchphrases.

Roddenberry: Gene Roddenberry, creator of "Star Trek," a groundbreaking science fiction series.

Smart: Maxwell Smart from "Get Smart," a bumbling secret agent known for his catchphrase "Missed it by that much."

Solo: Napoleon Solo from "The Man from U.N.C.L.E.," a suave and skilled secret agent.

Spock: Mr. Spock from "Star Trek," known for his logical thinking and pointed ears.

Tate: Larry Tate from "Bewitched," Darrin's boss at the advertising agency.

Van Dyke: Dick Van Dyke, known for his comedic role in "The Dick Van Dyke Show."

CINEMA - 15 trivia

Welcome to the dazzling era of 1960s cinema, a time when Hollywood blossomed under the golden Californian sun, setting the silver screen ablaze with groundbreaking films, legendary directors, and charismatic stars. This was a decade of innovation and revolution, both in the art of movie-making and in the stories that flickered to life in darkened theaters across the world.

In the 1960s, Hollywood stood at the crossroads of the traditional and the new, navigating the shifting tides of cultural change. The decade began under the lingering influence of the Golden Age of Hollywood, with its glamorous stars and studio-driven productions. Yet, it rapidly evolved, embracing more daring narratives, stylistic experimentation, and a newfound boldness in storytelling. This was the era that challenged norms, broke barriers, and redefined what cinema could be.

The decade saw the emergence of films that would become cornerstones of cinematic history. Directors like Alfred Hitchcock, Stanley Kubrick, and David Lean pushed the boundaries of the film medium. Hitchcock's "Psycho" sent shockwaves with its psychological thrills, while Kubrick's "2001: A Space Odyssey" took audiences on an unparalleled journey through space and time. Lean's epic "Lawrence of Arabia" painted the screen with its breathtaking desert vistas.

Iconic actors and actresses became household names, their performances etching themselves into the annals of film history. The charm of Audrey Hepburn in "Breakfast at Tiffany's," the raw intensity of Paul Newman in "Butch Cassidy and the Sundance Kid," and the captivating Elizabeth Taylor in "Cleopatra" are just a few examples of the era's unforgettable talents.

As we turn the pages to explore this vibrant decade, we've compiled a series of quizzes to test your knowledge and rekindle your love for 60s cinema. These questions will guide you through a journey of the most successful movies, directors, and actors/actresses of the time. From the stirring melodies of "The Sound of Music" to the wild west of "The Good, the Bad and the Ugly," and the enigmatic charm of James Bond in "Goldfinger," each question is an invitation to revisit the classics and relive the magic of 60s Hollywood.

So, grab your popcorn, settle into your seat, and let's rewind the film reel. It's time to immerse ourselves in the unforgettable atmosphere of 1960s cinema – an era that reshaped the world of movies and left an indelible mark on the hearts of cinephiles everywhere. Lights, camera, action!

1. What significant technical innovation was introduced with the 1968 film "2001: A Space Odyssey" directed by Stanley Kubrick?

A) Use of CGI

B) Advanced sound editing

C) Introduction of Steadicam

D) Special effects for space scenes

E) 3D film technology

2. Which film, released in 1969, is credited with initiating the "New Hollywood" phase and the modern Western genre?

A) The Wild Bunch

B) Butch Cassidy and the Sundance Kid

C) True Grit

D) The Magnificent Seven

E) Easy Rider

3. Who became the first African American to win the Academy Award for Best Actor in 1963?

A) Sidney Poitier

B) James Earl Jones

C) Harry Belafonte

D) Morgan Freeman

E) Denzel Washington

4. Which 1967 film is considered a landmark in cinema for its portrayal of race relations and is known for the famous line, "They call me Mr. Tibbs!"?

A) In the Heat of the Night

B) Guess Who's Coming to Dinner

C) To Sir, with Love

D) The Graduate

E) Bonnie and Clyde

5. Which 1962 film starring Gregory Peck is noted for addressing the issue of racism in the American South?

A) To Kill a Mockingbird

B) Cape Fear

C) The Guns of Navarone

D) Roman Holiday

E) Moby Dick

6. Who directed the epic historical drama "Lawrence of Arabia" which was released in 1962?

A) Alfred Hitchcock

B) Stanley Kubrick

C) David Lean

D) John Ford

E) Orson Welles

7. Which 1960 film is famous for its pioneering use of the jump cut, influencing future editing techniques?

A) Breathless

B) The Apartment

C) Psycho

D) Spartacus

E) La Dolce Vita

8. What 1964 musical film, set in the early 1900s, reflects the social changes happening in the 1960s?

A) West Side Story

B) My Fair Lady

C) Mary Poppins

D) The Sound of Music

E) Funny Girl

9. Which actress won an Academy Award for her debut film performance in "Mary Poppins" (1964)?

A) Audrey Hepburn

B) Julie Andrews

C) Elizabeth Taylor

D) Sophia Loren

E) Natalie Wood

10. What 1963 film is notable for its early and innovative use of split-screen technique?

A) The Great Escape

B) Cleopatra

C) Hud

D) The Pink Panther

E) The Cardinal

11. Which film won the Academy Award for Best Picture in 1961 and was a significant musical of the era?

A) West Side Story

B) The Apartment

C) Lawrence of Arabia

D) Ben-Hur

E) My Fair Lady

12. Who played Eliza Doolittle in "My Fair Lady"?

A. Audrey Hepburn

B. Julie Andrews

C. Elizabeth Taylor

D. Vivien Leigh

E. Grace Kelly

13. Which influential director made his feature film directorial debut with "Fear and Desire" in 1964?

A) Stanley Kubrick

B) Roman Polanski

C) Francis Ford Coppola

D) Martin Scorsese

E) Steven Spielberg

14. Which 1960 film, directed by Billy Wilder, is known for its satirical take on corporate culture and the American workplace?

A) The Apartment

B) Some Like It Hot

C) Psycho

D) Breakfast at Tiffany's

E) The Hustler

15. Which actress delivered an Oscar-winning performance in the 1962 film "Hud," establishing herself as a major talent in Hollywood?

A) Patricia Neal

B) Audrey Hepburn

C) Elizabeth Taylor

D) Katharine Hepburn

E) Sophia Loren

Psycho

The 1960s film "Psycho," directed by the legendary Alfred Hitchcock, is renowned for its suspense and psychological intrigue. One of the most iconic scenes in cinema history is the shower scene, where the character Marion Crane, played by Janet Leigh, is shockingly murdered. A fascinating anecdote about this scene is the use of chocolate syrup to simulate blood, as the film was shot in black and white. The choice of chocolate syrup was due to its realistic texture and contrast on black and white film. Additionally, the film's infamous shower scene was composed of over 70 camera shots and 50 cuts, a groundbreaking and meticulous editing technique at the time. This scene took an entire week to shoot, a significant portion of the film's overall shooting schedule. The careful crafting of this scene, combined with Bernard Herrmann's eerie music score, created one of the most memorable and terrifying moments in film history, forever changing the thriller genre.

Crucipuzzle N. 9
Hidden Words: A 1962 political thriller film starring Frank Sinatra, Angela Lansbury and Laurence Harvey.

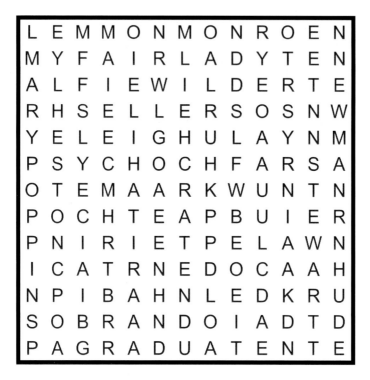

```
L E M M O N M O N R O E N
M Y F A I R L A D Y T E N
A L F I E W I L D E R T E
R H S E L L E R S O S N W
Y E L E I G H U L A Y N M
P S Y C H O C H F A R S A
O T E M A A R K W U N T N
P O C H T E A P B U I E R
P N I R I E T P E L A W N
I C A T R N E D O C A A H
N P I B A H N L E D K R U
S O B R A N D O I A D T D
P A G R A D U A T E N T E
```

Alfie: A 1966 British romantic comedy-drama film, known for its portrayal of the swinging sixties in London.

Brando: Marlon Brando, an actor known for his powerful performances and method acting, notably in "The Godfather."

Breakfast: "Breakfast at Tiffany's," a 1961 romantic comedy film starring Audrey Hepburn.

Dean: James Dean, an iconic actor symbolizing youthful rebellion, known for "Rebel Without a Cause."

Graduate: "The Graduate," a 1967 film known for its social themes and Simon & Garfunkel's soundtrack.

Grant: Cary Grant, a leading actor known for his charm in romantic comedies and thrillers.

Hepburn: Audrey Hepburn, known for her roles in "Breakfast at Tiffany's" and "My Fair Lady."

Heston: Charlton Heston, known for his epic roles, including that in "Ben-Hur."

Hud: A 1963 film starring Paul Newman, known for its modern Western themes.

Leigh: Vivien Leigh, an actress known for her dramatic performances, including in "Gone with the Wind."

Lemmon: Jack Lemmon, an actor known for his roles in comedies and dramas, including "The Apartment."

Lolita: A 1962 film directed by Stanley Kubrick, based on the novel by Vladimir Nabokov.

Loren: Sophia Loren, an actress known for her beauty and performances in Italian and American films.

Mary Poppins: A 1964 musical fantasy film featuring a magical nanny who transforms the lives of a London family, known for its iconic songs and Julie Andrews' performance in the title role.

Monroe: Marilyn Monroe, a symbol of Hollywood glamour and a popular actress of the era.

My Fair Lady: A 1964 musical film known for its songs and Audrey Hepburn's role as Eliza Doolittle.

Newman: Paul Newman, known for his charismatic performances and roles in films like "Cool Hand Luke."

Peck: Gregory Peck, known for his roles in dramas, including "To Kill a Mockingbird."

Poitier: Sidney Poitier, the first African American to win the Academy Award for Best Actor.

Psycho: A 1960 Alfred Hitchcock film, famous for its suspense and the iconic shower scene.

Sellers: Peter Sellers, an actor known for his versatile performances, including in "Dr. Strangelove."

Spartacus: A 1960 epic historical drama film directed by Stanley Kubrick.

Stewart: James Stewart, known for his everyman roles in various genres, including Westerns and thrillers.

Wayne: John Wayne, an actor known for his roles in Westerns and as an American icon.

Wilder: Billy Wilder, a director known for his sharp wit and successful films across genres.

SPORT - 25 trivia

Step into the vibrant and dynamic world of 1960s sports, an era where athleticism and cultural shifts intertwined, creating a tapestry of memorable moments and legendary figures. This was a decade marked by immense change, not just in society but on the playing fields, courts, tracks, and rings where sports history was written.

In the United States, the 1960s were a golden era for sports, with baseball, football, and basketball capturing the nation's imagination like never before. Baseball, America's pastime, was dominated by towering figures like Mickey Mantle, whose prowess with the New York Yankees made him a household name. The Los Angeles Dodgers' Sandy Koufax and Don Drysdale pitched their way into the annals of baseball history with their unmatched skill and finesse.

The decade also witnessed the rise of the National Football League (NFL.. with stars like Johnny Unitas of the Baltimore Colts and Bart Starr of the Green Bay Packers exemplifying excellence and leadership. Meanwhile, the National Basketball Association (NBA. saw its own legends take center stage. Bill Russell of the Boston Celtics and Wilt Chamberlain of the Philadelphia 76ers became symbols of greatness in the sport, their rivalry defining a generation.

Outside of team sports, the 60s shone a spotlight on individual greatness. In the boxing ring, Muhammad Ali's charisma and prowess made him an icon not just in sports but in global culture. The golfing world was mesmerized by the rivalry between Arnold Palmer and Jack Nicklaus, whose battles on the greens became the stuff of legend. And in the world of auto racing, names like Richard Petty and A.J. Foyt roared into history with their high-speed exploits.

As we delve into the quizzes that follow, we invite you to test your knowledge of these icons and the moments that made them legends. From the record-setting feats on the track and field to the slam dunks, home runs, and touchdown passes that had fans on the edge of their seats, these questions cover the spectrum of 60s sports glory. Each question is a window into a past filled with excitement, passion, and the pursuit of greatness.

So lace up your sneakers, grab your glove, and get ready to relive the thrilling world of 1960s sports. Whether you're a lifelong fan or new to the legends of this era, these quizzes offer a fun and engaging way to explore the athletic achievements that shaped a decade and left an indelible mark on the history of sports. Let's dive into the action and excitement that defined an unforgettable era in sports history!

1. Who set the MLB record for most home runs in a single season in 1961, breaking Babe Ruth's longstanding record?

A. Mickey Mantle

B. Hank Aaron

C. Willie Mays

D. Roger Maris

E. Ted Williams

2. In 1966, which NFL team won their first-ever Super Bowl, marking the start of their dominance in the sport?

A. Green Bay Packers

B. Dallas Cowboys

C. Pittsburgh Steelers

D. Kansas City Chiefs

E. New York Jets

3. Which boxer famously declared, "I am the greatest" and "I shook up the world" after winning the World Heavyweight Championship in 1964?

A. Joe Frazier

B. Sonny Liston

C. George Foreman

D. Muhammad Ali

E. Floyd Patterson

4. What significant event happened in the 1960 Winter Olympics held in Squaw Valley, USA?

A. First use of artificial snow in the Olympics

B. The USA won their first hockey gold medal

C. Introduction of the biathlon

D. Debut of the luge event

E. First Winter Olympics to be televised live

5. Which athlete broke the color barrier in professional golf by competing in the Masters Tournament in 1961?

A. Charlie Sifford

B. Calvin Peete

C. Lee Elder

D. Tiger Woods

E. Gary Player

6. Who won the Triple Crown of Thoroughbred Racing in 1966, becoming the first horse to do so in 25 years?

A. Northern Dancer

B. Secretariat

C. Affirmed

D. Seattle Slew

E. American Pharoah

7. Which female tennis player won the Grand Slam (winning all four major championships in a single calendar year) in 1962 and 1969?

A. Billie Jean King

B. Margaret Court

C. Chris Evert

D. Maria Bueno

E. Martina Navratilova

8. In the 1968 Summer Olympics, who set a world record in the long jump that stood for almost 23 years?

A. Carl Lewis

B. Jesse Owens

C. Bob Beamon

D. Mike Powell

E. Ralph Boston

9. Which NFL player was known as "The Kansas Comet" and set numerous rookie records in 1965?

A. Jim Brown

B. Gale Sayers

C. Walter Payton

D. Emmitt Smith

E. Barry Sanders

10. What was the major achievement of Wilt Chamberlain in an NBA game in 1962?

A. Scoring 100 points in a single game

B. Achieving a quadruple-double

C. Winning both the MVP and Defensive Player of the Year

D. Scoring the most three-pointers in a game

E. Breaking the record for most rebounds in a game

11. Hockey - Boston Bruins: Which legendary defenseman began his career with the Boston Bruins in the 1960s?

A. Bobby Orr

B. Wayne Gretzky

C. Gordie Howe

D. Ray Bourque

E. Mario Lemieux

12. Baseball - Los Angeles Dodgers: Which legendary pitcher for the Los Angeles Dodgers pitched a perfect game in 1965?

A. Sandy Koufax

B. Don Drysdale

C. Clayton Kershaw

D. Fernando Valenzuela

E. Orel Hershiser

13. Basketball - San Francisco Warriors: Who was a key player for the San Francisco Warriors in the 1960s?

A. Nate Thurmond

B. Wilt Chamberlain

C. Rick Barry

D. Chris Mullin

E. Stephen Curry

14. Football - Oakland Raiders: Which quarterback led the Oakland Raiders in the late 1960s?

A. Daryle Lamonica

B. Ken Stabler

C. Jim Plunkett

D. Rich Gannon

E. Derek Carr

15. Boxing: Who won the heavyweight boxing title in 1964 and later became known as Muhammad Ali?

A. Floyd Patterson

B. Joe Frazier

C. George Foreman

D. Sonny Liston

E. Cassius Clay

The Fosbury Flop

One of the most iconic moments in 1960s American sports occurred during the 1968 Summer Olympics in Mexico City, in the realm of athletics. It was on the high jump track where Dick Fosbury revolutionized the sport. Before Fosbury, high jumpers used techniques like the straddle method or the scissors jump. But Fosbury introduced what came to be known as the "Fosbury Flop." He would run at the bar, turn his back, and arch over it headfirst and backwards, a technique initially considered bizarre and ineffective by many. However, Fosbury proved skeptics wrong when he won the gold medal, setting a new Olympic record at 2.24 meters (7 ft 4 in.. His innovative technique not only earned him a place on the podium but also changed the high jump forever. Today, the Fosbury Flop is the standard technique used by high jumpers around the world, a lasting legacy of Fosbury's daring and ingenuity at the 1968 Olympics.

----

16. Golf: Who won the Masters Tournament in 1960, 1962, 1964, and 1978?

A. Jack Nicklaus

B. Arnold Palmer

C. Gary Player

D. Lee Trevino

E. Ben Hogan

17. Track and Field: Who set the world record in the mile run in 1966?

A. Jim Ryun

B. Steve Prefontaine

C. Sebastian Coe

D. Roger Bannister

E. Emil Zátopek

18. Decathlon: Who won the gold medal in the decathlon at the 1960 Summer Olympics?

A. Rafer Johnson

B. Bruce Jenner (Caitlyn Jenner.

C. Daley Thompson

D. Bill Toomey

E. Bob Mathias

19. College Football - USC Trojans: Which Heisman Trophy-winning running back played for USC in the late 1960s?

A. O.J. Simpson

B. Reggie Bush

C. Marcus Allen

D. Charles White

E. Anthony Davis

20. College Basketball - UCLA Bruins: Who was the star player for UCLA under coach John Wooden, known then as Lew Alcindor?

A. Kareem Abdul-Jabbar

B. Bill Walton

C. Gail Goodrich

D. Marques Johnson

E. Sidney Wicks

21. NASCAR: Who was a dominant NASCAR driver in the late 1950s and 1960s, known as "The King"?

A. Richard Petty

B. Dale Earnhardt

C. Jeff Gordon

D. Jimmie Johnson

E. Tony Stewart

22. Tennis: Who was the first African-American male to win a Grand Slam title, achieving this at the US Open in 1968?

A. Arthur Ashe

B. Althea Gibson

C. Serena Williams

D. Venus Williams

E. Yannick Noah

23. Golf: Which golfer, known for his rivalry with Arnold Palmer, won the U.S. Open in 1962, 1967, and 1972?

A. Jack Nicklaus

B. Gary Player

C. Lee Trevino

D. Sam Snead

E. Ben Hogan

24. Auto Racing - IndyCar: Who is a famous IndyCar driver, known for winning the Indianapolis 500 four times?

A. A.J. Foyt

B. Mario Andretti

C. Dan Gurney

D. Bobby Unser

E. Al Unser

25. Tennis: Which female tennis player won 24 Grand Slam singles titles, including six times at the Australian Open in the 1960s?

A. Billie Jean King

B. Margaret Court

C. Martina Navratilova

D. Steffi Graf

E. Chris Evert

Crucipuzzle N. 10

Hidden Words: A dominant basketball player known for scoring 100 points in a single NBA game

```
M A Y S N A M A T H W I L
T O N W M I K I T A N R O
R F O L I L L Y P E R R Y
B R O C K W O R R A K M A
B A F R O B E R T S O N N
E Z L C L R O S E B U H Y
L I O I I M U M T U F A A
I E J M V A N C B N A S Z
V R O E A R I C B N X P R
E S P O S I T O E I L I H
A A R O N S A V N N A T O
U S A Y E R S E C G I Z W
C L A R K E N Y H U L L E
```

Aaron: Hank Aaron, a legendary baseball player known for breaking Babe Ruth's home run record.

Ali: Muhammad Ali, a heavyweight boxer famous for his prowess in the ring and his charismatic personality.

Beliveau: Jean Beliveau, a Canadian ice hockey player known for his leadership with the Montreal Canadiens.

Bench: Johnny Bench, a baseball catcher known for his power hitting and exceptional defensive skills.

Brock: Lou Brock, a baseball player known for his base-stealing prowess and speed.

Brown: Jim Brown, a football running back known for his record-setting nine-year career with the Cleveland Browns.

Bunning: Jim Bunning, a baseball pitcher known for his no-hitters and perfect game.

Clarke: Bobby Clarke, a Canadian ice hockey player known for his leadership and aggressive play.

Esposito: Phil Esposito, a hockey center known for his scoring ability.

FloJo: Florence Griffith Joyner, an American track and field athlete known for her speed and unique style.

Frazier: Joe Frazier, a heavyweight boxer known for his powerful left hook and rivalry with Muhammad Ali.

Howe: Gordie Howe, a Canadian ice hockey player known for his scoring talent and longevity in the sport.

Hull: Bobby Hull, a Canadian ice hockey player known for his fast skating and powerful shot.

Koufax: Sandy Koufax, a baseball pitcher known for his

dominating performances and multiple no-hitters.

Lilly: Bob Lilly, a football defensive tackle known for his strength and agility.

Maris: Roger Maris, a baseball player known for breaking Babe Ruth's single-season home run record.

Mays: Willie Mays, a baseball center fielder known for his exceptional all-around skills.

McCovey: Willie McCovey, a baseball first baseman known for his powerful hitting.

Mikita: Stan Mikita, a Canadian ice hockey player known for his scoring and playmaking abilities.

Namath: Joe Namath, a football quarterback known for his charismatic personality and Super Bowl III victory.

Nicklaus: Jack Nicklaus, a professional golfer known for his numerous major championship wins.

Oliva: Tony Oliva, a baseball right fielder known for his batting skills.

Orr: Bobby Orr, a Canadian ice hockey player known for revolutionizing the defenseman position.

Perry: Gaylord Perry, a baseball pitcher known for his use of the spitball.

Robertson: Oscar Robertson, a basketball player known for being the first to average a triple-double for a season.

Rose: Pete Rose, a baseball player known for his hitting records and hustle on the field.

Sayers: Gale Sayers, a football running back known for his agility and elusiveness.

Spitz: Mark Spitz, an Olympic swimmer known for winning seven gold medals in a single Olympics.

Starr: Bart Starr, a football quarterback known for his leadership with the Green Bay Packers.

Unitas: Johnny Unitas, a football quarterback known for his record-setting performances and late-game heroics.

West: Jerry West, a basketball player known for his scoring ability and the silhouette on the NBA logo.

Yaz: Carl "Yaz" Yastrzemski, a baseball legend, primarily associated with the Boston Red Sox, known for his remarkable hitting and outfield skills, and he's often affectionately referred to as "Yaz."

LITERATURE & ART - 30 trivia

Welcome to the vibrant and transformative world of the 1960s, a decade where art and literature not only mirrored the rapid changes in society but also helped to propel them. This was a time of bold experimentation, political and social upheaval, and groundbreaking creativity that left an indelible mark on the cultural landscape.

In the realm of visual arts, the 1960s was a period of dazzling diversity and innovation. Artists like Andy Warhol and Roy Lichtenstein became the faces of Pop Art, transforming everyday objects and comic strips into high art and challenging traditional notions of artistic expression.

Meanwhile, the abstract expressionism of Jackson Pollock and Mark Rothko invited viewers into worlds of emotive color and form, redefining the boundaries of the canvas.

The world of architecture witnessed revolutionary ideas taking physical form. Jorn Utzon's Sydney Opera House emerged as an architectural marvel, its majestic sails becoming a global icon of imaginative design. Moshe Safdie's Habitat 67 in Montreal reimagined urban living, while Eero Saarinen's TWA Flight Center at JFK Airport embodied the spirit of the Space Age with its futuristic curves.

Literature in the 1960s was equally dynamic, with novelists exploring new realms of narrative and theme. The decade saw the rise of influential writers like Harper Lee, whose "To Kill a Mockingbird" offered a profound commentary on racial injustice. The satirical genius of Joseph Heller's "Catch-22" and the magical realism of Gabriel García Márquez's "One Hundred Years of Solitude" expanded the horizons of literary fiction. Meanwhile, Sylvia Plath's "The Bell Jar" delved into the depths of mental illness with poignant clarity.

As we venture into the quizzes that follow, we invite you to explore the masterpieces and minds that shaped this extraordinary decade. From the colorful canvases of Pop Art to the profound pages of groundbreaking novels, and the visionary structures that redefined cityscapes, these questions will guide you through a journey of discovery and appreciation. Each query is not just a test of knowledge but an invitation to experience the revolutionary spirit and creative fervor of the 1960s.

So, let your imagination take flight as we delve into the artistic and literary wonders of an era that continues to inspire and intrigue. It's time to rediscover the 60s, a decade that danced to the rhythm of change and painted its dreams in bold strokes.

143

1. "To Kill a Mockingbird" by Harper Lee (1960.: Who is the narrator of the story?

A. Atticus Finch

B. Scout Finch

C. Tom Robinson

D. Boo Radley

E. Jem Finch

2. "Catch-22" by Joseph Heller (1961.: What is the name of the protagonist who struggles with the paradoxical rules of war?

A. Milo Minderbinder

B. Yossarian

C. Nately

D. Colonel Cathcart

E. Orr

3. "Franny and Zooey" by J.D. Salinger (1961.: What is the primary focus of Franny's spiritual crisis in the book?

A. Love and Relationships

B. The Jesus Prayer

C. Family Dynamics

D. Academic Pressure

E. Fame and Success

4. "A House for Mr Biswas" by V.S. Naipaul (1961.: What is the lifelong goal of the protagonist, Mr. Biswas?

A. To become wealthy

B. To write a novel

C. To own a house

D. To travel the world

E. To find true love

5. "The Prime of Miss Jean Brodie" by Muriel Spark (1961.: Miss Jean Brodie is a teacher at which type of school?

A. A public school in London

B. A girls' school in Edinburgh

C. A university in Oxford

D. A boarding school in the countryside

E. A high school in New York

6. "A Clockwork Orange" by Anthony Burgess (1962.: What is the main character, Alex, known for?

A. His musical talent

B. His love for classical literature

C. Leading a gang of delinquents

D. Being a political activist

E. His skills in chess

7. "Pale Fire" by Vladimir Nabokov (1962.: The novel "Pale Fire" is presented as a commentary on a poem written by which character?

A. Charles Kinbote

B. John Shade

C. Sybil Shade

D. Dr. Charles Xavier

E. Gerald Emerald

8. "One Flew Over the Cuckoo's Nest" by Ken Kesey (1962.: Who is the tyrannical nurse in the psychiatric hospital?

A. Nurse Ratched

B. Nurse Bloom

C. Nurse Fletcher

D. Nurse Barton

E. Nurse Dawson

9. "The Bell Jar" by Sylvia Plath (1963.: What is the profession of the protagonist, Esther Greenwood?

A. Teacher

B. Journalist

C. Nurse

D. Poet

E. Actress

10. "Cat's Cradle" by Kurt Vonnegut (1963.: What is the name of the fictional substance that can freeze water at room temperature in "Cat's Cradle"?

A. Ice-Nine

B. Frostium

C. Chillite

D. Subzeroxin

E. Arctic Compound

11. "V." by Thomas Pynchon (1963.: What is the mysterious entity that the novel's characters seek?

A. A rare diamond

B. A secret society

C. A lost city

D. A person or place known as "V."

E. A hidden treasure

12. "Herzog" by Saul Bellow (1964.: What does Moses Herzog do throughout the novel?

A. Travels the world

B. Writes letters to famous people

C. Runs for political office

D. Searches for a lost artifact

E. Teaches at a university

13. "The Spy Who Came In from the Cold" by John le Carré (1964.: Who is the main character, a British intelligence officer?

A. George Smiley

B. Alec Leamas

C. James Bond

D. Jack Ryan

E. Harry Palmer

14. "Dune" by Frank Herbert (1965.: On which desert planet is the novel predominantly set?

A. Tatooine

B. Arrakis

C. Krypton

D. Vulcan

E. Pandora

15. "In Cold Blood" by Truman Capote (1966.: What event does the book explore?

A. The Watergate scandal

B. The assassination of JFK

C. The Clutter family murders

D. The Cuban Missile Crisis

E. The Moon landing

The Secret Plan to Nuke the Moon

In the height of the Cold War and space race, the United States conceived an audacious and now almost unbelievable plan known as 'Project A119'. The objective was staggering: to detonate a nuclear bomb on the Moon. Initiated in the late 1950s and continuing into the early 1960s, this top-secret project aimed to demonstrate American superiority in space over the Soviet Union. The explosion was intended to be visible from Earth, serving as a display of strength and technological prowess. However, the project was eventually abandoned due to the potential risk of radioactive fallout, the uncertain scientific outcomes, and the moral implications of such an aggressive act. The existence of Project A119 remained classified for decades, only coming to light in the late 20th century, revealing a startling chapter in the history of the space race that could have altered our view of the Moon forever.

----

16. "The Crying of Lot 49" by Thomas Pynchon (1966.: What is the protagonist, Oedipa Maas, trying to uncover?

A. A family secret

B. The truth about a corporate conspiracy

C. The existence of an underground postal system

D. The location of a missing person

E. The meaning of a mysterious painting

17. "Wide Sargasso Sea" by Jean Rhys (1966.: Who is the protagonist, serving as a prequel character to "Jane Eyre"?

A. Jane Eyre

B. Antoinette Cosway

C. Mr. Rochester

D. Bertha Mason

E. St. John Rivers

18. "One Hundred Years of Solitude" by Gabriel García Márquez (1967.: Which family's multi-generational story is chronicled in the novel?

A. The Buendía family

B. The Marquez family

C. The Garcia family

D. The Solitude family

E. The Urbino family

19. "The Master and Margarita" by Mikhail Bulgakov (1967.: Who visits Moscow in this novel, causing chaos and confusion?

A. A group of revolutionaries

B. The devil and his retinue

C. An alien spaceship

D. A lost tsar

E. A famous American actor

20. "Do Androids Dream of Electric Sheep?" by Philip K. Dick (1968.: What is Rick Deckard's profession?

A. A detective

B. An android designer

C. A bounty hunter

D. A spaceship pilot

E. A scientist

21. "Marilyn Diptych" by Andy Warhol (1962.: What technique did Warhol use in creating "Marilyn Diptych"?

A. Oil painting

B. Watercolor

C. Silkscreen printing

D. Charcoal drawing

E. Collage

22. "Whaam!" by Roy Lichtenstein (1963.: What was Lichtenstein's inspiration for "Whaam!"?

A. Abstract expressionism

B. Renaissance paintings

C. Comic book panels

D. Nature landscapes

E. Photographs

23. "No. 5/No. 22" by Mark Rothko (1964.: Rothko's "No. 5/No. 22" is known for its distinctive use of what?

A. Geometric shapes

B. Drip painting technique

C. Large blocks of color

D. Black and white contrast

E. Collage elements

24. "Convergence" by Jackson Pollock (1960.: What is the main technique used in Pollock's "Convergence"?

A. Pointillism

B. Drip painting

C. Fresco

D. Impasto

E. Encaustic painting

25. "Campbell's Soup Cans" by Andy Warhol (1962.: How many soup can variations did Warhol create in this series?

A. 10

B. 32

C. 50

D. 64

E. 100

26. "Three Flags" by Jasper Johns (1965.: What is the distinctive feature of Jasper Johns' "Three Flags"?

A. Three-dimensional texture

B. Use of metallic paint

C. Integration of photography

D. Layering of three canvases

E. Fluorescent colors

27. "Sydney Opera House" designed by Jørn Utzon (1960s.: What design element is the Sydney Opera House most famous for?

A. Its glass dome

B. The sail-like shells

C. The underwater auditorium

D. Its revolving stage

E. The use of gold leaf

28. "Habitat 67" in Montreal, designed by Moshe Safdie (1967.: What was the primary purpose of the "Habitat 67" design?

A. Luxury hotel

B. Government offices

C. Urban housing

D. Museum

E. Shopping center

29. "TWA Flight Center" at JFK Airport, designed by Eero Saarinen (1962.: What was the TWA Flight Center known for architecturally?

A. Its minimalist design

B. The use of traditional materials

C. Its futuristic design and curved forms

D. Gothic revival style

E. A pyramid shape

30. "Black Sun" by Isamu Noguchi (1960.: Where is the "Black Sun" sculpture located?

A. New York City

B. Seattle's Volunteer Park

C. Tokyo

D. Paris

E. Chicago

Katherine Johnson: The Mathematician Who Helped Reach the Stars

The 1960s marked a pivotal era in space exploration, and Katherine Johnson, an African-American mathematician at NASA, played a crucial role in it. Born in 1918 in West Virginia, Johnson showed an exceptional talent for mathematics from an early age, overcoming both gender and racial barriers in a field dominated by white men.

Her most significant contributions came during the space race of the 1960s, particularly with the Apollo 11 mission in 1969. Johnson's expertise in celestial navigation was instrumental in calculating the trajectory for the first human spaceflight to the Moon. Her precise calculations ensured the safe return of the astronauts, cementing her role in this historic achievement.

Despite working in a segregated NASA, Johnson's skills and determination earned her respect and recognition amongst her peers. Her story remained relatively unknown until the 2016 film "Hidden Figures" brought her remarkable achievements to light.

Katherine Johnson's legacy is not only in her mathematical genius but also in her trailblazing role as a woman of color in science, inspiring countless others to pursue their dreams regardless of societal boundaries.

Crucipuzzle N. 11

Hidden Words: The acclaimed autobiography of writer Maya Angelou (1969).

Adams: Celebrated photographer known for his striking black-and-white landscape photographs.

Albee: Playwright known for works like "Who's Afraid of Virginia Woolf?"

Baldwin: Eminent novelist and social critic, author of "Giovanni's Room."

Bellow: Nobel Prize-winning novelist, author of "Herzog."

Didion: Writer known for her lucid prose style and incisive depictions of social unrest and psychological fragmentation.

Dylan: Iconic singer-songwriter known for his influential music in the 1960s.

Evans: Photographer known for his work documenting the effects of the Great Depression.

Flavin: Artist known for creating sculptural objects and installations from commercially available fluorescent light fixtures.

Frank: Influential photographer and filmmaker, best known for his book "The Americans."

Gaddis: Writer known for his complex, lengthy novels like "The Recognitions."

Hesse: Sculptor known for pioneering work in materials like latex, fiberglass, and plastics.

Hopper: Painter known for his introspective and moody depictions of American life.

Jasper: Artist known for his minimalist and geometric paintings and sculptures.

Johns: Artist known for his paintings and prints that play on images of flags, maps, and targets.

LeWitt: Artist who became prominent for his wall drawings and "structures" (a term he preferred instead of "sculptures".

Morris: Sculptor, conceptual artist, and writer, a key figure in the minimalist movement.

O'Keeffe: Painter known for her large-scale, close-up paintings of flowers.

Oldenburg: Sculptor known for his public art installations and soft sculptures.

Penn: Influential photographer known for his fashion, portrait, and still life images.

Plath: Poet and author of "The Bell Jar," known for her confessional style of poetry.

Pynchon: Novelist known for his dense and complex novels.

Roth: Novelist known for his 1960s novel "Portnoy's Complaint."

Salinger: Author of "The Catcher in the Rye," a defining novel of teenage disillusionment.

Smith: Photographer, photojournalist known for his major photo essays.

Sontag: Writer and filmmaker, best known for her essays on modern culture.

Stella: Painter known for his works of concentric squares and half-circles in a wide range of colors.

Twombly: Artist known for his large-scale, freely scribbled, calligraphic-style graffiti paintings.

Updike: Novelist and short story writer, known for his "Rabbit" series

CARTOONS AND COMICS - 20 trivia

A Colorful Era of Imagination – Cartoons and Comics of the 1960s

In this chapter, we journey into an era where animation and comic strips were not just a source of entertainment but also a reflection of the changing times, resonating with kids and adults alike.

The 1960s were a period of cultural transformation, and this was vividly mirrored in the animated shows and comic books of the time. This was the decade that introduced the world to the charm of "The Flintstones," a modern stone-age family that brought laughter into living rooms across

America. It was a time when "The Jetsons" gave us a whimsical glimpse into the future, and superheroes like Spider-Man and The X-Men leaped from the comic pages, capturing the imagination of a generation.

Television during the 60s saw an explosion of colorful characters. Shows like "Scooby-Doo" combined mystery and humor, creating a recipe that delighted kids every Saturday morning. Meanwhile, the comic book industry saw a surge in creativity, with Marvel Comics introducing complex characters and narratives that challenged the traditional norms of superhero storytelling.

The 60s were also a time of innovation in animation techniques and storytelling. The era saw the emergence of anime in Japan, with shows like "Astro Boy" marking the beginning of a global phenomenon. In the United States, animation studios experimented with new styles and themes, pushing the boundaries of what cartoons could be.

As you dive into the quizzes that follow, you'll rediscover the iconic characters and stories that defined the 1960s. From the adventures of superheroes to the everyday humor of comic strip families, each question will take you on a nostalgic journey through a decade rich in creativity and imagination.

So, let's set the dial to the swinging sixties, where every flip of a comic book page and every turn of a TV channel brought a new world of wonder and excitement. Get ready to explore an era where cartoons and comics were a vibrant tapestry of color, creativity, and cultural expression!

1. "The Flintstones" (1960.: What is the name of Fred Flintstone's wife?

A. Wilma

B. Betty

C. Pebbles

D. Daphne

E. Barbara

2. "The Jetsons" (1962.: What is the name of the Jetsons' family dog?

A. Astro

B. Comet

C. Rocket

D. Pluto

E. Luna

3. "Jonny Quest" (1964.: What is the name of Jonny's best friend and companion?

A. Bandit

B. Max

C. Spike

D. Hadji

E. Toto

4. "Scooby-Doo. Where Are You!" (1969.: What is the name of the van used by the Mystery Inc. gang?

A. Mystery Wagon

B. Ghost Chaser

C. Scooby Van

162

D. The Mystery Machine

E. Adventure Mobile

5. "The New Adventures of Superman" (1966.: What is Superman's alter ego?

A. Bruce Wayne

B. Peter Parker

C. Clark Kent

D. Tony Stark

E. Steve Rogers

6. "The Amazing Spider-Man" by Stan Lee and Steve Ditko (1962.: Who is Spider-Man's primary love interest in the early comics?

A. Mary Jane Watson

B. Gwen Stacy

C. Felicia Hardy

D. Susan Storm

E. Lois Lane

7. "X-Men" by Stan Lee and Jack Kirby (1963.: Who is the founder and leader of the X-Men?

A. Wolverine

B. Cyclops

C. Professor X

D. Magneto

E. Storm

8. "The Avengers" by Stan Lee and Jack Kirby (1963.: Which character is a founding member of the Avengers?

A. Spider-Man

B. Thor

C. Black Panther

D. Doctor Strange

E. The Falcon

9. "Fantastic Four" by Stan Lee and Jack Kirby (1961.: What is the name of the Fantastic Four's leader, who can stretch his body?

A. The Human Torch

B. The Thing

C. Mr. Fantastic

D. Invisible Woman

E. Dr. Doom

10. "Green Lantern" (reintroduction. by John Broome and Gil Kane (1960.: What is the real name of the Silver Age Green Lantern?

A. Bruce Wayne

B. Hal Jordan

C. Barry Allen

D. Clark Kent

E. Tony Stark

11. Top Cat" (1961.: What is the name of the police officer who is always trying to catch Top Cat and his gang?

A. Officer Dibble

B. Sergeant Snagglepuss

C. Captain Canine

D. Detective Dogg

E. Constable Cat

12. "Magilla Gorilla" (1964.: What type of store is Magilla Gorilla for sale in?

A. Toy store

B. Grocery store

C. Pet store

D. Antique store

E. Book store

13. "Atom Ant" (1965.: What is Atom Ant's main superpower?

A. Invisibility

B. Super strength and speed

C. Ability to fly

D. Laser vision

E. Time travel

14. "Secret Squirrel" (1965.: What is the name of Secret Squirrel's sidekick?

A. Morocco Mole

B. Agent Mouse

C. Spy Squirrel

D. Undercover Otter

E. Mystery Mongoose

15. "Space Ghost" (1966.: What are the names of Space Ghost's teenage sidekicks?

A. Jan and Jace

B. Ken and Kara

C. Sam and Sally

D. Tim and Tina

E. Nick and Nora

16. "The Adventures of Batman" (1968.: Who is Batman's sidekick in this animated series?

A. Robin

B. Batgirl

C. Nightwing

D. Alfred

E. The Joker

17. "Frosty the Snowman" (1969.: What brings Frosty the Snowman to life in this animated special?

A. A magic hat

B. Snow on Christmas Eve

C. A child's wish

D. A spell

E. A solar eclipse

18. "Pink Panther" (1969.: What is the primary focus of the Pink Panther cartoon series?

A. Solving mysteries

B. Stealing diamonds

C. Causing mischief

D. Protecting the jungle

E. Searching for food

19. "Dastardly and Muttley in Their Flying Machines" (1969.: What is the main objective of Dastardly and Muttley in the series?

A. To win races

B. To catch a pigeon

C. To find treasure

D. To escape from an island

E. To save the world

20. "The Incredible Hulk" by Stan Lee and Jack Kirby (1962.: What triggers Bruce Banner's transformation into the Hulk?

A. Full moon

B. Anger and stress

C. Magic spell

D. Exposure to water

E. Sound waves

CRUCIPUZZLE 12

Hidden Words: The first TV special based on the comic strip Peanuts.

```
M B A M M B A M M X S I A
C A R N O L D H I W C R T
G T R A R J T L L I O O O
E M I V E N E W B L O N P
R A R O I F V T E E B M C
A N W T O N L I S E Y A A
L S N O O P Y U S O T N T
D I G S M U R F C I N Y R
T A N T M A N N L Y O O C
M A Q U A M A N H A H N M
R I C A S P E R S T S O T
B U L L W I N K L E T H M
W O N D E R W O M A N A S
```

Ant-Man: Marvel superhero with the ability to shrink in size.

Aquaman: DC Comics superhero and ruler of the underwater kingdom of Atlantis.

Arnold: From "The Magic Slate," known for his interactions with the unseen narrator.

Atom: DC Comics superhero with the ability to shrink his body to varying degrees.

Bamm-Bamm: The Flintstones' super-strong toddler neighbor.

Batman: DC Comics superhero and protector of Gotham City.

Bullwinkle: A goofy moose from "The Rocky and Bullwinkle Show."

Casper: A friendly ghost who seeks to make friends rather than scare people.

Felix: A classic animated character known for his magic bag of tricks.

Flash: DC Comics superhero known for his superhuman speed.

Gerald: From "Gerald McBoing-Boing," known for communicating with sound effects.

Iron Man: Marvel Comics superhero known for his advanced suit of armor.

Jetson: The main character from "The Jetsons," depicting a family in a futuristic world.

Lucy: From "Peanuts," known for her psychiatric booth and pulling the football away from Charlie Brown.

Linus: The blanket-carrying philosopher from "Peanuts."

Magoo: Elderly, wealthy, short-sighted cartoon character.

Marvin: The Martian from Looney Tunes, known for his attempts to destroy Earth.

Scooby: A talking Great Dane known for solving mysteries with his human companions.

Smurf: Tiny blue creatures living in a village and constantly thwarting Gargamel.

Snoopy: The imaginative beagle from "Peanuts."

Tintin: A young reporter known for his adventures with his dog Snowy.

Thor: Marvel's Asgardian God of Thunder, wielding a powerful hammer.

Top Cat: The charismatic alley cat leader of a gang of streetwise cats.

Tweety: The innocent but smart yellow canary often pursued by Sylvester.

Vision: A synthetic humanoid and superhero in Marvel Comics.

Wile E.: The perpetually failing coyote in pursuit of the Road Runner.

Wonder Woman: DC Comics superheroine, an Amazonian princess.

SCIENCE - 10 trivia

Step into the exhilarating world of 1960s science, an era that stands as a testament to human curiosity and ingenuity. This decade was a crucible of discovery and innovation, where boundaries were pushed, and new frontiers were boldly explored. In these transformative years, science was not just a pursuit of knowledge; it was a thrilling adventure into the unknown.

In the realm of physics, the 1960s were illuminated by the groundbreaking proposal of quarks by Murray Gell-Mann and George Zweig. These fundamental particles, hidden deep within the atom's nucleus, opened up a new understanding of the subatomic world. Meanwhile, in the skies above, the space race reached its zenith. The first human spaceflight by Yuri Gagarin and the Apollo Moon Landing by NASA were not just triumphs of engineering; they were symbols of humanity's eternal dream to reach for the stars.

The decade was also a time of remarkable medical advances. The first successful human-to-human heart transplant by Dr. Christiaan Barnard in 1967 was a marvel that pushed the boundaries of surgery. In the quiet realm of laboratories, the intricacies of DNA's replication mechanisms were unraveled, deepening our understanding of the blueprint of life.

Technological innovation was on a rapid ascent, with Theodore Maiman's creation of the first working laser igniting possibilities that would transform medicine, communication, and technology. The invention and refinement of integrated circuits laid the foundation for the digital revolution that was to follow, forever changing the landscape of computing and electronics.

As we embark on the quizzes that follow, prepare to dive into a world where every discovery was a headline, and every breakthrough a leap into the future. From the depths of the Earth's crust, where plate tectonics reshaped our understanding of the planet, to the far reaches of space, where the first close-up pictures of Mars captured our imagination, the 1960s were a testament to the relentless pursuit of knowledge.

So, let's journey back to this remarkable era, where science was not just a subject to be studied but a thrilling narrative of progress and discovery. Uncover the stories, the people, and the inventions that made the 1960s a landmark decade in the annals of scientific history.

1. Who is credited with proposing the existence of quarks?

A. Niels Bohr and Werner Heisenberg

B. James Watson and Francis Crick

C. Murray Gell-Mann and George Zweig

D. Albert Einstein and Max Planck

E. Richard Feynman and Paul Dirac

2. What was the first type of laser invented by Theodore Maiman?

A. Gas laser

B. Semiconductor laser

C. Fiber laser

D. Dye laser

E. Ruby laser

3. Who was the first human to journey into outer space?

A. Neil Armstrong

B. John Glenn

C. Yuri Gagarin

D. Buzz Aldrin

E. Alan Shepard

4. Who discovered the cosmic microwave background radiation?

A. Edwin Hubble and Georges Lemaître

B. Stephen Hawking and Roger Penrose

C. Arno Penzias and Robert Wilson

D. Carl Sagan and Frank Drake

E. Fred Hoyle and Thomas Gold

5. Who performed the first successful human-to-human heart transplant?

A. Michael DeBakey

B. Joseph Murray

C. Christiaan Barnard

D. Norman Shumway

E. Denton Cooley

6. Which spacecraft transmitted the first close-up pictures of Mars?

A. Voyager 1

B. Mariner 4

C. Pioneer 10

D. Viking 1

E. Galileo

7. Who discovered pulsars, rapidly rotating neutron stars?

A. Jocelyn Bell Burnell and Antony Hewish

B. Carl Sagan and Edwin Salpeter

C. Stephen Hawking and Roger Penrose

D. Subrahmanyan Chandrasekhar and William Fowler

E. Vera Rubin and Kent Ford

8. Who is credited with the invention of the integrated circuit?

A. Tim Berners-Lee and Robert Noyce

B. Jack Kilby and Robert Noyce

C. Bill Gates and Paul Allen

D. Steve Jobs and Steve Wozniak

E. Gordon Moore and Andrew Grove

9. Valium was primarily used to treat what condition?

A. Diabetes

B. Anxiety

C. High blood pressure

D. Asthma

E. Arthritis

10. Which medical technology was first developed in the 1960s and later became a crucial tool in diagnostic imaging?

A. Magnetic Resonance Imaging (MRI.

B. Computed Tomography (CT. scan

C. Ultrasound imaging

D. Positron Emission Tomography (PET.

E. Electrocardiogram (ECG.

_____

The LED Revolution: A Quiet Breakthrough

One of the most impactful yet underappreciated technological advancements of the 1960s was the invention of the Light Emitting Diode (LED.. In 1962, Nick Holonyak Jr., an engineer at General Electric, developed the first practical visible-spectrum LED. Initially producing only red light, LEDs were a groundbreaking development in semiconductor and lighting technology.

Holonyak's invention was a significant leap forward from earlier versions of the diode, which emitted infrared light and were mainly used in circuitry and as indicator lamps. The introduction of the visible-spectrum LED opened up a myriad of possibilities. By the late 1960s, LEDs were being integrated into calculators, digital watches, and test equipment, heralding a new era of electronic displays.

Though their usage was initially limited due to high production costs and low intensity, the foundational work in the 1960s set the stage for the LEDs' widespread application in later decades. Today, LEDs are ubiquitous, found in everything from energy-efficient household lighting to digital screens, medical devices, and even space exploration technology. The LED is a prime example of a quiet revolution in the 1960s that profoundly transformed the technological landscape, laying the groundwork for advancements in energy efficiency, longevity, and the miniaturization of electronic components.

_____

Crucipuzzle N. 13
Hidden Words: Nobel Prize in Physics in 1965

Alvarez: Physicist known for his work on the hydrogen bubble chamber and the theory on dinosaur extinction.

Bethe: Physicist who won the Nobel Prize for his work on the theory of nuclear reactions.

Bohm: Made significant contributions to quantum theory and neuropsychology.

Bohr: Pioneering figure in quantum theory and nuclear physics.

Born: Nobel laureate recognized for his fundamental research in Quantum Mechanics.

Chandrasekhar: Astrophysicist known for the Chandrasekhar limit in white dwarf theory.

Crick: Co-discoverer of the structure of DNA.

Dirac: Made fundamental contributions to the early development of both quantum mechanics and quantum electrodynamics.

Dyson: Theoretical physicist and mathematician known for his work in quantum electrodynamics and solid-state physics.

Einstein: Developed the theory of relativity, a pillar of modern physics.

Fermi: Created the world's first nuclear reactor; key figure in the development of quantum theory and nuclear and particle physics.

Gamow: Theoretical physicist and cosmologist, significantly contributed to the Big Bang theory.

Gell-Mann: Physicist who proposed the quark model in particle physics.

Glaser - Physicist who invented the bubble chamber, a device used to track electrically charged particles, for which he received the Nobel Prize in Physics.

Land: Inventor and co-founder of Polaroid Corporation.

Leakey: Paleoanthropologist who made significant findings on human evolution.

Pauling: Chemist known for his work in quantum chemistry and molecular biology.

Rabi: Physicist recognized for his discovery of nuclear magnetic resonance.

Rubin: Astronomer who pioneered work on galaxy rotation rates.

Salk: Medical researcher who developed the first successful polio vaccine.

Schwinger: Theoretical physicist, known for his work on quantum electrodynamics.

Shockley: Co-inventor of the transistor and Nobel laureate in Physics.

Teller: Theoretical physicist, known as the "father of the hydrogen bomb."

Tomonaga: Physicist who significantly advanced quantum electrodynamics.

Townes: Physicist who played a major role in the development of lasers.

Watson: Co-discoverer of the structure of DNA.

Wigner: Physicist and mathematician, known for his contributions to nuclear physics, quantum mechanics, and quantum field theory.

Yukawa: Theoretical physicist, the first to predict the existence of mesons.

MUSIC - 25 trivia

The Harmonic Revolution – Music of the 1960s

Welcome to the 1960s, a decade of musical exploration and cultural revolution. This was an era that sang the songs of change, where the rhythms of rebellion and the melodies of freedom resonated through the air. In this chapter, we'll dive into the heart of the '60s, exploring the music that defined a generation and left an indelible mark on the world.

The 1960s was a time when music was more than just entertainment; it was a powerful force for social and political expression. It was the decade of The Beatles, whose innovative sounds and styles captivated millions and transformed the landscape of popular music. Bands like The Rolling Stones, The Beach Boys, and The Who brought new energy and edge to rock music, while Bob Dylan's poetic lyrics gave voice to the counterculture movement.

This era also saw the rise of soul and Motown, with artists like Aretha Franklin, James Brown, and The Supremes delivering powerful performances that still resonate today. The decade was marked by iconic music festivals like Woodstock, symbolizing peace, love, and music, and bringing together a generation in celebration.

From the psychedelic sounds of Jimi Hendrix and Janis Joplin to the smooth harmonies of Simon & Garfunkel, the music of the '60s was as diverse as it was influential. It was a time when every chord struck a chord, every beat told a story, and every lyric echoed the hopes and dreams of a generation.

As we journey through a series of quizzes on the music of the 1960s, you'll have the opportunity to rediscover the songs that became anthems, the artists who became legends, and the moments that defined an era. Each question is a window into the past, a glimpse into a decade that reshaped music forever. So, let's rewind the tape, turn up the volume, and immerse ourselves in the unforgettable soundtrack of the 1960s!

1. Who sang the groundbreaking song "Like a Rolling Stone" in 1965?

A. Bob Dylan

B. Neil Young

C. Leonard Cohen

D. Van Morrison

E. Bruce Springsteen

2. Which band released the hit song "I Want to Hold Your Hand" in 1964?

A. The Beatles

B. The Rolling Stones

C. The Beach Boys

D. The Who

E. The Kinks

3. "Respect," a powerful anthem for both the civil rights and feminist movements, was sung by...

A. Aretha Franklin

B. Diana Ross

C. Tina Turner

D. Etta James

E. Janis Joplin

4. Which group is known for the song "(I Can't Get No. Satisfaction"?

A. The Beatles

B. The Rolling Stones

C. Led Zeppelin

D. The Kinks

E. The Animals

5. "Good Vibrations," a song known for its innovative production, was by which band?

A. The Beach Boys

B. The Beatles

C. The Byrds

D. The Mamas & the Papas

E. The Moody Blues

6. "Hey Jude," a song featuring a famous sing-along outro, was performed by...

A. The Beatles

B. Elton John

C. Bob Dylan

D. The Rolling Stones

E. Pink Floyd

7. "Light My Fire," a hit that contributed to the rise of psychedelic rock, was by...

A. The Doors

B. Jefferson Airplane

C. Grateful Dead

D. Jimi Hendrix

E. Janis Joplin

8. "My Girl," a classic Motown hit, was recorded by which group?

A. The Temptations

B. The Four Tops

C. The Supremes

D. Smokey Robinson & The Miracles

E. The Jackson 5

9. "A Change Is Gonna Come," a song symbolizing hope and change, was sung by...

A. Sam Cooke

B. Marvin Gaye

C. Otis Redding

D. Ray Charles

E. James Brown

10. "Purple Haze," a song known for its innovative guitar work, was performed by...

A. Jimi Hendrix

B. Eric Clapton

C. Keith Richards

D. Jimmy Page

E. Pete Townshend

11. Which song by The Beatles is famous for its final, extended piano chord?

A. "Hey Jude"

B. "Let It Be"

C. "A Day in the Life"

D. "Yesterday"

E. "Come Together"

12. "I Heard It Through the Grapevine" was a hit for which artist in 1968?

A. Otis Redding

B. Marvin Gaye

C. Sam Cooke

D. James Brown

E. Stevie Wonder

13. Who released the song "Stand by Me" in 1961?

A. Ben E. King

B. Otis Redding

C. Marvin Gaye

D. Sam Cooke

E. Ray Charles

14. "All Along the Watchtower" is a song famously covered by which artist?

A. Jimi Hendrix

B. Bob Dylan

C. Eric Clapton

D. Janis Joplin

E. Neil Young

15. "California Dreamin'" was a popular song by which group?

A. The Mamas & the Papas

B. The Beach Boys

C. Simon & Garfunkel

D. The Byrds

E. The Lovin' Spoonful

16. Which song by The Rolling Stones was released in 1968 and is known for its sambalike rhythm?

A. "Paint It Black"

B. "Sympathy for the Devil"

C. "Gimme Shelter"

D. "(I Can't Get No. Satisfaction"

E. "You Can't Always Get What You Want"

17. "What's Going On," a song addressing various social issues, was released by...

A. Marvin Gaye

B. Stevie Wonder

C. James Brown

D. Curtis Mayfield

E. Al Green

18. "Space Oddity," a song about an astronaut named Major Tom, was by...

A. David Bowie

B. Elton John

C. Pink Floyd

D. The Beatles

E. The Rolling Stones

19. The song "The House of the Rising Sun," famously covered by The Animals, is a...

A. Traditional folk song

B. Rock and roll original

C. Jazz standard

D. Blues classic

E. Pop tune

20. "Sunshine of Your Love," a song known for its distinctive guitar riff, was performed by...

A. Cream

B. The Jimi Hendrix Experience

C. Led Zeppelin

D. The Who

E. Pink Floyd

21. Which famous guitarist founded the band The Experience in 1965?

A. Eric Clapton

B. Jimi Hendrix

C. Jeff Beck

D. Keith Richards

E. George Harrison

22. What is the name of the folk music trio known for the hit "Leaving on a Jet Plane"?

A. The Mamas & the Papas

B. Peter, Paul, and Mary

C. Simon & Garfunkel

D. The Kingston Trio

E. Crosby, Stills, Nash & Young

23. Which band released the album "Freak Out!" considered as one of the first concept albums?

A. The Beatles

B. Pink Floyd

C. The Mothers of Invention (Frank Zappa..

D. The Velvet Underground

E. The Who

24. What was the name of the venue in San Francisco that became synonymous with the "San Francisco Sound" in the 1960s?

A. The Fillmore

B. Winterland Ballroom

C. The Avalon Ballroom

D. The Matrix

E. The Warfield

25. Which band released the hit song "White Rabbit" in 1967?

A. The Doors

B. The Grateful Dead

C. Jefferson Airplane

D. Pink Floyd

E. Cream

Crucipuzzle N. 14
Hidden Words: A Nancy Sinatra hit from 1966

```
C P M C L E A N C T C C R
A A A H N S U P R E M E S
S T R A E S C H E R N E K
H S L E D G E B A O E O I
O Y E C O O K E M T L S N
D A Y R E D D I N G S R K
O E F O U R S E A S O N S
O R B I S O N S T O N E S
R M A D Z E P P E L I N G
S D R E F R A N K L I N E
E Y A R D B I R D S I Y F
B B U F F A L O O K A R W
A L B E A T L E S G K I N
```

Baez (Joan. - Folk singer known for her distinctive voice and political activism.

Beatles - Legendary British band that led the 'British Invasion' of the US music scene.

Buffalo - Band known for pioneering the country rock and Americana genres.

Byrds - American band that merged folk music with rock and roll.

Cash (Johnny. - Iconic country singer known for hits like "Folsom Prison Blues."

CCR (Creedence Clearwater Revival. - Influential rock band with a string of hits including "Bad Moon Rising."

Cher - Singer and actress known for her distinctive voice and versatility.

Cooke (Sam. - Influential soul singer known for songs like "A Change Is Gonna Come."

Cream - British rock supergroup known for hits like "Sunshine of Your Love."

Doors - Influential rock band known for their poetic lyrics and charismatic frontman.

Dylan - Influential singer-songwriter known for his poetic lyrics and social commentary.

Four Seasons - American rock and pop band known for their distinctive harmonies and hit songs like "December, 1963 (Oh, What a Night." and "Sherry."

Franklin (Aretha. - Powerful soul singer known for her emotive voice and civil rights activism.

Gaye (Marvin. - Soul singer known for his smooth voice and hits like "What's Going On."

King (Carole. - Prolific songwriter and singer, known for her album "Tapestry."

Kinks - British rock band known for their influential sound and hit songs like "You Really Got Me."

Marley (Bob. - Jamaican singer-songwriter who became an international icon of reggae music.

McLean (song "American Pie". - Don McLean's epic song reflecting America's cultural changes.

Nelson (Willie. - Country music singer known for his unique voice and outlaw country style.

Orbison (Roy. - Singer known for his distinctive, impassioned voice and dark, emotional ballads.

Patsy (Cline. - Country music singer known for her smooth, emotive voice.

Redding (Otis. - Influential soul singer known for his passionate, gritty voice.

Simone (Nina. - Singer known for her musical versatility and civil rights activism.

Sledge (song "When a Man Loves a Woman". - Percy Sledge's soulful ballad, a classic in R&B music.

Stones (Rolling Stones. - Pioneering rock band known for their bluesy sound and longevity.

Supremes - Premier Motown girl group known for their string of hits.

Yardbirds - British rock band known for their experimental approach to blues rock.

Zeppelin (Led Zeppelin. - Influential rock band known for their heavy sound and epic compositions.

THE FIFTIES

a)   TELEVISION (PROGRAMS AND TV SERIES. 25 trivia

QUESTION N.	CORRECT ANSWER
1	B. Starring in "I Love Lucy" Lucille Ball became a television icon for her role in "I Love Lucy," a sitcom that aired from 1951 to 1957. The show was a major milestone in American TV history, known for its humor and pioneering use of a three-camera setup.
2	A. Ricky Ricardo Desi Arnaz played Ricky Ricardo, the husband of Lucy Ricardo (Lucille Ball. in "I Love Lucy." The show was also groundbreaking for featuring an interracial marriage, reflecting Arnaz's own Cuban heritage.
3	A. Mr. Television Milton Berle was nicknamed "Mr. Television" during TV's golden age. He was one of the first major American TV stars, hosting NBC's "Texaco Star Theatre" from 1948 to 1956.
4	B. Your Show of Shows Sid Caesar was best known for "Your Show of Shows," which aired from 1950 to 1954. The show was a landmark in American comedy and influenced many future TV sketch shows.
5	A. The Honeymooners Jackie Gleason's most famous role was as Ralph Kramden in "The Honeymooners." The show, originally a sketch within "The Jackie Gleason Show," became a standalone series in 1955.

QUESTIO N N.	CORRECT ANSWER
6	B. Hosting "The Bob Hope Show" Bob Hope was famous for hosting "The Bob Hope Show," a variety series that aired from 1952 to 1955. He was known for his quick wit and was also a prominent figure in USO tours.
7	A. The Twilight Zone Rod Serling created "The Twilight Zone," an anthology series known for its clever plot twists, science fiction themes, and social commentary. It first aired in 1959 and became a seminal work in TV history.
8	A. The Ed Sullivan Show Ed Sullivan hosted "The Ed Sullivan Show," a variety series that ran from 1948 to 1971. The show was famous for featuring a diverse range of entertainers and was a staple of American Sunday night television.
9	C. His variety show Red Skelton was known for "The Red Skelton Show," a variety show that showcased his talents as a comedian and actor. The show ran from 1951 to 1971 and was loved for its characters and sketches.
10	B. Norton in "The Honeymooners" Art Carney played Ed Norton, the best friend and neighbor of Ralph Kramden (Jackie Gleason) in "The Honeymooners." His performance is celebrated for its comedic timing and chemistry with Gleason.
11	B. The Honeymooners Audrey Meadows played Alice Kramden, the wife of Ralph Kramden (Jackie Gleason), in "The Honeymooners." She was known for her strong-willed and level-headed character
12	B. Variety show Dinah Shore was famous for "The Dinah Shore Chevy Show," a variety series that aired from 1956

QUESTIO N N.	CORRECT ANSWER
	to 1963. She was known for her singing talent and charming personality.
13	B. Variety show host Explanation: Perry Como was known for hosting "The Perry Como Show," a variety series that aired from 1948 to 1963. He was a popular crooner and TV personality, known for his relaxed singing style.
14	C. The George Burns and Gracie Allen Show George Burns and Gracie Allen starred in "The George Burns and Gracie Allen Show," a sitcom that aired from 1950 to 1958. The show was known for breaking the fourth wall, with Burns often speaking directly to the audience.
15	B. Variety show Jack Benny was known for "The Jack Benny Program," a variety show that aired from 1950 to 1965. Benny was celebrated for his comedic timing and his ability to play a comedic "tightwad" character.
16	B. George Reeves George Reeves famously portrayed Superman in the 1950s television series "Adventures of Superman."
17	B. Cowboy "Cheyenne," starring Clint Walker, followed the adventures of Cheyenne Bodie, a cowboy roaming the American West.
18	B. Husband and Wife George Burns and Gracie Allen played a married couple, mirroring their real-life marriage, in "The George Burns and Gracie Allen Show"
19	A. Trigger Roy Rogers' palomino horse, Trigger, was a well-known and beloved character on "The Roy Rogers Show."
20	B. Donna Reed

QUESTIO N N.	CORRECT ANSWER
	Donna Reed starred as Donna Stone, the matriarch of the Stone family, in "The Donna Reed Show."
21	A. High School Teacher "Our Miss Brooks," starring Eve Arden, was about a witty high school English teacher named Connie Brooks.
22	A. Hugh O'Brian Hugh O'Brian starred as the legendary lawman Wyatt Earp in this Western television series.
23	A. Dodge City, Kansas The series initially set in Dodge City, Kansas, follows the life of Wyatt Earp before moving to Tombstone, Arizona.
24	A. Dale Evans Dale Evans played the role of Dale Evans, often riding alongside Roy Rogers in the series.
25	B. A strong, independent female lead "Our Miss Brooks" was ahead of its time, showcasing a female lead character who was both independent and career-oriented.

b)   CINEMA 15 trivia

QUESTIO N N.	CORRECT ANSWER
1	A. Alfred Hitchcock "Rear Window" was directed by Alfred Hitchcock, known for his mastery in suspense and psychological thriller genres.
2	B. James Dean James Dean starred in "Rebel Without a Cause," a film that became a symbol of youth rebellion.
3	A. Audrey Hepburn

QUESTIO N N.	CORRECT ANSWER
	Audrey Hepburn's performance in "Roman Holiday" made her a star and won her an Academy Award for Best Actress.
4	C. Singin' in the Rain "Singin' in the Rain" is known for its iconic song and dance number by Gene Kelly.
5	A. Humphrey Bogart Humphrey Bogart played Charlie Allnut in "The African Queen," for which he won his only Oscar.
6	A. Vivien Leigh Vivien Leigh's portrayal of Blanche DuBois in "A Streetcar Named Desire" is one of her most acclaimed roles.
7	A. Gloria Swanson Gloria Swanson gave a memorable performance as Norma Desmond in "Sunset Boulevard."
8	D. The Girl Marilyn Monroe's character is famously known as "The Girl" in "The Seven Year Itch."
9	B. Alec Guinness Alec Guinness played Colonel Nicholson in "The Bridge on the River Kwai," a role that earned him an Academy Award.
10	A. Billy Wilder "Some Like It Hot," a classic comedy, was directed by Billy Wilder.
11	A. Marlon Brando Marlon Brando's iconic role as Terry Malloy in "On the Waterfront" earned him an Oscar.
12	A. Alan Ladd Alan Ladd starred as the mysterious gunfighter Shane in this classic Western
13	A. Cecil B. DeMille Cecil B. DeMille directed "The Ten Commandments," known for its epic scale and

QUESTIO N N.	CORRECT ANSWER
	grandeur.
14	B. Kim Novak Kim Novak played the dual roles of Madeleine Elster and Judy Barton in Hitchcock's "Vertigo."
15	B. James Dean "East of Eden" was James Dean's first major film role, earning him critical acclaim

c)   SPORT 25 trivia

QUESTIO N N.	CORRECT ANSWER
1	A. New York Yankees Joe DiMaggio played his entire 13-year baseball career for the New York Yankees.
2	A. Brooklyn Dodgers Jackie Robinson famously broke the color barrier in MLB when he started playing for the Brooklyn Dodgers in 1947.
3	C. Outfielder Mickey Mantle was primarily an outfielder during his career with the New York Yankees
4	B. New York Giants Willie Mays played for the New York Giants before the team moved to San Francisco
5	A. New York Yankees Yogi Berra played for the New York Yankees and was one of the most famous catchers in baseball history.
6	A. Boston Red Sox Ted Williams played his entire career with the Boston Red Sox and is considered one of the greatest hitters in baseball history.
7	A. Milwaukee Braves Hank Aaron started his MLB career with the

QUESTION N.	CORRECT ANSWER
	Milwaukee Braves before the team relocated to Atlanta.
8	A. St. Louis Cardinals Stan Musial played his entire 22-year career with the St. Louis Cardinals.
9	A. Milwaukee Braves Warren Spahn, one of the greatest left-handed pitchers, played the majority of his career with the Milwaukee Braves.
10	A. Cleveland Indians Bob Feller, a Hall of Fame pitcher, played his entire career with the Cleveland Indians.
11	A. Sugar Ray Robinson Sugar Ray Robinson, considered one of the greatest boxers of all time, held the world middleweight title five times.
12	D. Heavyweight Rocky Marciano was an undefeated heavyweight champion known for his powerful punching.
13	A. 21 Floyd Patterson became the youngest heavyweight champion at age 21 in 1956.
14	B. 9 years Archie Moore was the light heavyweight world champion for 9 consecutive years from 1952 to 1961.
15	B. Welterweight Carmen Basilio was a prominent figure in the welterweight class, known for his two victories over Sugar Ray Robinson
16	A. Boston Celtics Bill Russell played his entire career with the Boston Celtics, where he became one of the greatest basketball players of all time.
17	A. Philadelphia/San Francisco Warriors

QUESTIO N N.	CORRECT ANSWER
	Wilt Chamberlain started his NBA career with the Philadelphia Warriors, which later became the San Francisco Warriors.
18	B. Minneapolis/Los Angeles Lakers Elgin Baylor played for the Minneapolis Lakers, which later relocated to become the Los Angeles Lakers.
19	A. Johnny Unitas Johnny Unitas, quarterback for the Baltimore Colts, was nicknamed "The Golden Arm" for his exceptional passing skills.
20	A. Montreal Canadiens Maurice "Rocket" Richard spent his entire NHL career with the Montreal Canadiens and was one of the league's most prolific scorers
21	A. First African American to win Wimbledon Althea Gibson broke barriers as the first African American to win a Grand Slam title, including Wimbledon in 1957.
22	D. Decathlon Bob Mathias was a legendary decathlete, winning two Olympic gold medals in the decathlon in 1948 and 1952.
23	A. Mickey Mantle Mickey Mantle, one of the greatest switch-hitters in baseball history, was nicknamed "The Commerce Comet" after his hometown of Commerce, Oklahoma
24	A. Tennis Pancho Gonzales was one of the top tennis players in the 1950s, known for his powerful serve and competitive spirit.
25	A. Rocky Marciano Explanation: Rocky Marciano was the heavyweight champion who remained undefeated throughout his career in the 1950s, retiring with a

QUESTIO N N.	CORRECT ANSWER
	perfect record

d) LITERATURE & ART 30 trivia

QUESTIO N N.	CORRECT ANSWER
1	B. Jack In "Lord of the Flies," Jack Merridew is initially the leader of the choirboys and later becomes the leader of a group of boys on the island, symbolizing savagery and the desire for power.
2	C. Spider In "Charlotte's Web," Charlotte is a clever and caring spider who befriends Wilbur, a pig, and helps save him from being slaughtered.
3	B. Dolores "Lolita" Haze The narrator of "Lolita," Humbert Humbert, is infatuated and obsessively in love with a young girl, Dolores Haze, whom he nicknames "Lolita."
4	C. World War II "Night" is Elie Wiesel's memoir detailing his and his father's survival in the Auschwitz and Buchenwald concentration camps during the Holocaust in World War II.
5	D. Aslan Aslan, a lion, is a central character and the true king of Narnia in C.S. Lewis's "The Chronicles of Narnia." He is a symbol of goodness and righteousness.
6	B. Mouse Algernon is a laboratory mouse who has undergone surgery to increase his intelligence in "Flowers for Algernon." His progress parallels that of the main character, Charlie.

QUESTIO N N.	CORRECT ANSWER
7	C. Mars "The Martian Chronicles" by Ray Bradbury is a collection of interconnected stories primarily set on the planet Mars, focusing on the colonization and exploration of Mars and its impact
8	C. The Grinch The Grinch, a grouchy and solitary creature, is the main character in "How the Grinch Stole Christmas!" who attempts to prevent Christmas from coming to the town of Whoville
9	B. The Salem Witch Trials Arthur Miller's "The Crucible" is a dramatized account of the Salem witch trials that occurred in the Massachusetts Bay Colony, serving as an allegory for McCarthyism in the United States.
10	A. The clash between different cultures "Things Fall Apart" by Chinua Achebe deals with the impact of European colonialism in Africa, depicting the clash between traditional Igbo culture and the new values introduced by the colonizers
11	B. King Arthur "The Once and Future King" by T.H. White is a reimagining of the Arthurian legends, focusing on the life and reign of King Arthur.
12	A. Waiting for someone named Godot In Samuel Beckett's "Waiting for Godot," the characters Vladimir and Estragon spend the entire play waiting for the arrival of a mysterious figure named Godot.
13	C. A hill house "The Haunting of Hill House" is a gothic horror novel set in a mysterious old mansion known as Hill House, which is thought to be haunted.
14	C. Caspian In "The Voyage of the Dawn Treader," part of

QUESTIO N N.	CORRECT ANSWER
	"The Chronicles of Narnia" series, King Caspian is the young ruler of Narnia who embarks on a sea voyage to find seven lost lords.
15	A. The fall of an empire "Foundation" by Isaac Asimov is centered on the fall and eventual rise of a galactic empire. The story follows a group of scientists who seek to preserve knowledge and minimize the period of chaos
16	B. World War II "A Separate Peace" is set in a New England boarding school during World War II and explores themes of youth and innocence. war and rivalry.
17	C. A series of magical portals In "The Magician's Nephew." the Wood between the Worlds is a tranquil forest filled with pools that act as portals to different worlds, including Narnia and Earth.
18	C. Large blocks of color Mark Rothko is renowned for his large, abstract canvases featuring soft. rectangular forms floating on a stained field of color.
19	B. Abstract Expressionism Willem de Kooning was a leading figure in the Abstract Expressionist movement. known for his powerful, gestural style.
20	B. Everyday consumer goods Explanation: Andy Warhol is famously known for his paintings of everyday consumer goods. like Campbell's Soup Cans. reflecting his unique Pop Art style.
21	D. The Saturday Evening Post Norman Rockwell gained fame for his heartwarming and humorous illustrations for The Saturday Evening Post.

QUESTION N.	CORRECT ANSWER
22	C. Flowers and natural forms Georgia O'Keeffe is renowned for her paintings of enlarged flowers, New York skyscrapers, and New Mexico landscapes.
23	C. Mixed media artworks Robert Rauschenberg's "Combines" are innovative works that integrate aspects of painting and sculpture, blurring the line between art and everyday objects.
24	C. Flags Jasper Johns is known for incorporating images of flags, targets, numbers, and maps into his work, exploring how familiar symbols can convey multiple meanings.
25	D. Pop Art Roy Lichtenstein was a prominent figure in the Pop Art movement, famous for his comic strip-style paintings using a technique mimicking commercial printing
26	D. Silkscreen prints Andy Warhol's Marilyn Monroe series is notable for its silkscreen printing technique, which he used to produce brightly colored multiple images of the iconic actress
27	D. The Southwest Explanation: Georgia O'Keeffe is well-known for her paintings inspired by the landscape and natural forms of the American Southwest, particularly New Mexico
28	C. Fallingwater Explanation: Fallingwater, designed by Frank Lloyd Wright in 1935, is famous for its harmony with the surrounding landscape and the innovative way it extends over a waterfall
29	C. Modernism Explanation: Le Corbusier was a pioneer of

QUESTIO N N.	CORRECT ANSWER
	Modernism in architecture, known for his functionalist designs and innovative urban planning concepts
30	B. Yosemite National Park Explanation: Ansel Adams is renowned for his stunning black-and-white photographs of Yosemite National Park, which played a crucial role in promoting the conservation of this natural area

e) CARTOONS & COMICS 20 trivia

QUESTIO N N.	CORRECT ANSWER
1	E. An ordinary child with extraordinary intelligence "The Brain" was a comic series that centered around a character known as 'The Brain,' who was distinguished by his extraordinary intelligence and intellectual adventures
2	B. Mischievous child "Pat the Brat" was a comic strip centered around the antics and mischievous adventures of a young boy named Pat.
3	B. Everyday life of a young girl "Li'l Jinx" was a popular comic strip that humorously depicted the everyday life and misadventures of a little girl named Jinx
4	C. Archie Comics "Little Archie" was a spin-off of the popular "Archie Comics," featuring the adventures of Archie Andrews and his friends as children.
5	B. Humorous and child-friendly content "Melvin the Monster" was a comic strip known

QUESTIO N N.	CORRECT ANSWER
	for its light-hearted and humorous portrayal of a young monster named Melvin
6	B. Two babies and their adventures "Sugar and Spike" was a charming comic series that followed the adventures and mischiefs of two babies, Sugar Plumm and Cecil "Spike" Wilson
7	A. An angel living among humans "Little Angel" was a comic strip that revolved around the life of an angelic character living and interacting in the human world
8	A. Spoiled child with superpowers "Super Brat" was a comic strip about a spoiled child who had superpowers, often leading to humorous situations
9	B. A tomboyish girl and her daily life "Li'l Tomboy" was centered around a young, spirited girl who often defied traditional gender roles, focusing on her various escapades
10	B. A baby's imaginative adventures Explanation: "Little Ike" was a comic strip that depicted the imaginative and often humorous adventures of a baby named Ike
11	E. Magpies "The Heckle and Jeckle Show" featured two mischievous magpies known for their witty banter and humorous escapades
12	B. The Huckleberry Hound Show "The Yogi Bear Show" originated as a segment on "The Huckleberry Hound Show" before becoming a standalone show.
13	A. Super strength Mighty Mouse, the protagonist of the series, is known for his super strength and ability to fly, often saving the day with his powers.
14	E. Mr. Jinks

QUESTIO N N.	CORRECT ANSWER
	In "Pixie and Dixie and Mr. Jinks," the two mice, Pixie and Dixie, are often antagonized by Mr. Jinks, a cat who is perpetually frustrated by their antics
15	B. A dog Huckleberry Hound, the main character in "The Huckleberry Hound Show," is a blue dog known for his laid-back and drawling manner
16	D. Road Runner and Wile E. Coyote "The Road Runner Show" is famous for the endless chases between Road Runner and Wile E. Coyote, with the latter constantly devising elaborate but ultimately unsuccessful traps
17	B. Space exploration "The Ruff and Reddy Show," one of the first television cartoons produced by Hanna-Barbera, often featured space exploration themes with its main characters, Ruff (a cat. and Reddy (a dog..
18	B. Squirrel Explanation: "The Bullwinkle Show," also known as "Rocky and Bullwinkle," featured Bullwinkle, a dim-witted moose, and his clever friend, Rocky the Flying Squirrel
19	C. Near-sightedness Mr. Magoo is a wealthy, short-statured retiree who gets into various situations due to his extreme near-sightedness and refusal to admit the problem
20	A. Magic bag of tricks Explanation: Felix the Cat is a classic cartoon character known for his magical bag, which could assume various forms and functions to aid in his adventures.

f)   SCIENCE 10 trivia

QUESTIO N N.	CORRECT ANSWER
1	B. The double helix structure of DNA In 1953, Francis Crick and James Watson discovered the double helix structure of DNA. a fundamental breakthrough in understanding genetic information storage and transfer.
2	C. Charles Townes Although Theodore Maiman made the first operational laser in 1960, it was Charles Townes. along with Arthur Schawlow, who laid the theoretical groundwork in the late 1950s, leading to the development of the laser.
3	B. Development of the polio vaccine by Jonas Salk Jonas Salk developed the first successful polio vaccine in the 1950s, which was a major milestone in medical science. drastically reducing the incidence of poliomyelitis globally
4	C. Jack Kilby and Robert Noyce Jack Kilby and Robert Noyce independently invented the integrated circuit in the late 1950s, a technological breakthrough that led to the development of microchips and revolutionized electronics.
5	C. Walter Baade. In the early 1950s. Walter Baade significantly advanced our understanding of the Milky Way by distinguishing between two types of Cepheid variable stars. This led to more accurate distance measurements in the universe.
6	D. Observation of the muon neutrino The muon neutrino was first confirmed at Brookhaven National Laboratory in 1952,

QUESTION N.	CORRECT ANSWER
	marking a significant milestone in particle physics and the study of fundamental particles.
7	D. Explorer 3 Explorer 3, launched in 1957, played a crucial role in the discovery of the Van Allen radiation belt, a zone of energetic charged particles captured by Earth's magnetic field.
8	C. First successful kidney transplant Joseph Murray performed the first successful kidney transplant in 1954, a pioneering event in the field of organ transplantation.
9	C. Business data processing. UNIVAC I was notable for its role in business and administrative data processing, including usage in the U.S. Census Bureau.
10	C. Launch of Explorer 1 Explorer 1, the first American satellite, was launched in 1958. This event marked the beginning of the United States' entry into the Space Race.

g) MUSIC 25 trivia

QUESTION N.	CORRECT ANSWER
1	C. Chuck Berry. The song is one of his most famous and is a rock 'n' roll classic.
2	C. Elvis Presley. "Jailhouse Rock" is one of his most iconic songs
3	A. "What'd I Say." The song is famous for its electric piano intro and innovative sound

QUESTIO N N.	CORRECT ANSWER
4	A. One of the first rock 'n' roll records. The song was a massive hit and helped popularize rock 'n' roll.
5	C. Little Richard. "Tutti Frutti" is known for its energetic vocals and beat
6	B. Johnny Cash. The song is one of his signature hits
7	A. "That'll Be the Day." The song is one of their most popular and enduring hits
8	A. "Blueberry Hill." It's one of his most recognizable and beloved songs
9	D. Jerry Lee Lewis. The song is known for Lewis's energetic piano playing and vocals
10	A. Ritchie Valens. " La Bamba" is a rock 'n' roll adaptation of a traditional Mexican folk song
11	B. Elvis Presley. "Heartbreak Hotel" is one of Elvis's most famous songs and a key track in his early career.
12	A. "Long Tall Sally." The song is a classic example of Little Richard's dynamic and influential rock 'n' roll style
13	C. Bobby Darin. "Mack the Knife" showcased Darin's versatility as a vocalist and remains one of his most famous recordings.
14	B. Johnny Cash. The song is one of Cash's most iconic and enduring works.

QUESTION N.	CORRECT ANSWER
15	C. Buddy Holly. "Peggy Sue" is one of Holly's most memorable and beloved songs
16	A. Bill Haley & His Comets. The song was a major milestone in the popularization of rock and roll.
17	D. Jerry Lee Lewis. Known for his energetic piano playing, this song is one of his most famous.
18	C. Frankie Lymon & The Teenagers. The song is known for its doo-wop style and youthful energy.
19	A. Eddie Cochran. "Summertime Blues" is a classic rockabilly song reflecting teenage discontent and desire for freedom
20	A. Fats Domino. The song is one of his most recognized and enduring hits.
21	C. The Chords. "Sh-Boom" was a hit song by The Chords, considered one of the first successful doo-wop songs.
22	A. Big Mama Thornton The original version of "Hound Dog" was recorded by Big Mama Thornton in 1952, four years before Elvis Presley's version.
23	C. That's All Right. "That's All Right" was recorded by Elvis Presley in 1953 at Sun Studio. It is often regarded as one of the first rockabilly records, combining elements of blues and country music.
24	C. Songs for Lovers. Frank Sinatra's "Songs for Lovers" was the first album to top the newly established Billboard

QUESTIO N N.	CORRECT ANSWER
	album chart in 1956, marking a significant milestone in his career.
25	B. Martin Denny. Martin Denny was known as "The Father of Exotica," a genre characterized by its tropical-themed music that became popular in the 1950s. His music often featured unusual and exotic instruments.

THE SIXTIES

a. TELEVISION (PROGRAMS AND TV SERIES. 25 trivia

QUESTION N.	CORRECT ANSWER
1	A. Opie. Opie Taylor, played by Ron Howard, is the son of Sheriff Andy Taylor.
2	C. Comedy writer. Rob Petrie, played by Dick Van Dyke, is a comedy writer for a TV show.
3	D. Twitching her nose. Samantha, played by Elizabeth Montgomery, is known for her nose twitch to perform magic.
4	A. Texas. The Clampett family moves from a rural area in Texas after striking oil.
5	B. Ponderosa Ranch. The Cartwright family lives on the Ponderosa Ranch.
6	B. Rod Serling. Rod Serling was the creator and primary writer for The Twilight Zone.
7	C. Dr. McCoy. Dr. Leonard McCoy, also known as "Bones," is the chief medical officer.
8	B. Cesar Romero. Cesar Romero famously portrayed the Joker in the 1960s series.
9	B. On a beach. Tony Nelson, an astronaut, finds the bottle on a beach.
10	A. Vampire. Grandpa Munster is a vampire.
11	C. Seven. There were seven castaways on the S.S. Minnow.
12	A. The Beatles.

QUESTIO N N.	CORRECT ANSWER
	The Beatles made their U.S. television debut on The Ed Sullivan Show.
13	D. Murder. Dr. Kimble is wrongly accused of murdering his wife.
14	C. Maxwell Smart. Agent 86's real name is Maxwell Smart.
15	A. Emma Peel. Emma Peel, played by Diana Rigg, is John Steed's most iconic partner.
16	B. Stalag 13. The show is set in the fictional POW camp Stalag 13.
17	D. Defense lawyer. Raymond Burr famously portrayed the defense lawyer Perry Mason.
18	B. Lurch. The towering butler's name is Lurch.
19	B. Lawyer. Oliver was a lawyer before becoming a farmer in "Green Acres."
20	A. 714. Sergeant Joe Friday's badge number is famously 714.
21	B. B-9. The robot in "Lost in Space" is commonly referred to as the B-9.
22	A. Bedrock. The Flintstones reside in the town of Bedrock.
23	B. James Arness. James Arness played the iconic role of Marshal Matt Dillon.
24	C. Jim Phelps. Jim Phelps, played by Peter Graves, is the leader of the IMF team.

QUESTIO N N.	CORRECT ANSWER
25	C. Patrick Macnee. Patrick Macnee portrayed the debonair spy John Steed.

b.   CINEMA 15 trivia

QUESTIO N N.	CORRECT ANSWER
1	D) Special effects for space scenes "2001: A Space Odyssey" (1968) is celebrated for its pioneering special effects in depicting space and futuristic concepts, significantly influencing the science fiction genre.
2	B) Butch Cassidy and the Sundance Kid "Butch Cassidy and the Sundance Kid" (1969) played a pivotal role in defining the "New Hollywood" era and modernizing the Western genre with its style and narrative.
3	A) Sidney Poitier Sidney Poitier won the Academy Award for Best Actor in 1963 for his role in "Lilies of the Field," becoming the first African American to achieve this honor.
4	A) In the Heat of the Night "In the Heat of the Night" (1967) is noted for its progressive portrayal of race relations, particularly highlighted by the line, "They call me Mr. Tibbs!" delivered by Sidney Poitier's character.
5	A) To Kill a Mockingbird "To Kill a Mockingbird" (1962), featuring Gregory Peck, is renowned for its powerful

QUESTIO N N.	CORRECT ANSWER
	commentary on racism in the American South, based on the novel by Harper Lee.
6	C) David Lean David Lean directed "Lawrence of Arabia" (1962), an epic historical drama that is celebrated for its grand scale, cinematography, and direction.
7	A) Breathless "Breathless" (1960), directed by Jean-Luc Godard, is renowned for its innovative use of the jump cut, which profoundly influenced film editing techniques.
8	D) The Sound of Music "The Sound of Music" (1964) resonated with the 1960s audiences through its themes of nonconformity and resistance, mirroring the social changes of the era.
9	B) Julie Andrews Julie Andrews won the Academy Award for Best Actress for her debut film role in "Mary Poppins" (1964), marking a significant breakthrough in her career.
10	E) The Cardinal "The Cardinal" (1963) utilized the split-screen technique effectively, a novel approach at the time for showing simultaneous action in different locations.
11	A) West Side Story "West Side Story" (1961) won the Academy Award for Best Picture. It's renowned for its music and portrayal of urban issues, making it a significant musical of the era.
12	A) Elizabeth Taylor Elizabeth Taylor starred in the title role of "Cleopatra" (1963), a film famous for its grand scale and high budget.

QUESTIO N N.	CORRECT ANSWER
13	A) Stanley Kubrick Stanley Kubrick's directorial debut in feature films was with "Fear and Desire" in 1964, marking the beginning of his illustrious career.
14	A) The Apartment "The Apartment" (1960), directed by Billy Wilder, is acclaimed for its darkly comedic and satirical portrayal of corporate culture and the American workplace.
15	A) Patricia Neal Patricia Neal won the Academy Award for her performance in "Hud" (1962), marking her as a significant talent in Hollywood during that period.

c.   SPORT 25 trivia

QUESTIO N N.	CORRECT ANSWER
1	D. Roger Maris. He hit 61 home runs in 1961, surpassing Babe Ruth's record of 60.
2	A. Green Bay Packers. They won Super Bowl I in 1967 (for the 1966 season), under coach Vince Lombardi.
3	D. Muhammad Ali. He made these declarations after defeating Sonny Liston.
4	B. The USA won their first hockey gold medal.
5	A. Charlie Sifford.
6	D. Seattle Slew.
7	B. Margaret Court.

QUESTIO N N.	CORRECT ANSWER
8	C. Bob Beamon. His record-breaking jump was 8.90 meters (29 ft 2 ½ in).
9	B. Gale Sayers.
10	A. Scoring 100 points in a single game. He achieved this feat while playing for the Philadelphia Warriors
11	A. Bobby Orr. Orr started his NHL career with the Bruins and is considered one of the greatest defensemen in hockey history.
12	A. Sandy Koufax. Sandy Koufax pitched a perfect game on September 9, 1965, against the Chicago Cubs, cementing his status as one of the greatest pitchers in baseball history.
13	A. Nate Thurmond. Thurmond was a dominant player for the Warriors during that era.
14	A. Daryle Lamonica. Lamonica was known as "The Mad Bomber" for his deep-passing play style.
15	E. Cassius Clay. Cassius Clay changed his name to Muhammad Ali after winning the title.
16	B. Arnold Palmer. Palmer is one of golf's greatest players and had multiple Masters wins.
17	A. Jim Ryun. Ryun set the record as a high school student.
18	A. Rafer Johnson. Johnson's victory in 1960 was a highlight of his athletic career.
19	A. O.J. Simpson. Simpson won the Heisman in 1968.
20	A. Kareem Abdul-Jabbar.

QUESTIO N N.	CORRECT ANSWER
	Abdul-Jabbar played for UCLA as Lew Alcindor before changing his name.
21	A. Richard Petty. Petty is a NASCAR legend and was extremely successful during this period.
22	A. Arthur Ashe. Ashe's 1968 victory was a significant moment in tennis history.
23	A. Jack Nicklaus. Nicklaus is considered one of the greatest golfers of all time.
24	A. A.J. Foyt. Foyt's career spanned numerous decades, and he is a legend in IndyCar racing.
25	B. Margaret Court. Court's dominance in tennis included multiple wins at the Australian Open in the 1960s.

    d.   LITERATURE & ART 30 trivia

QUESTIO N N.	CORRECT ANSWER
1	B. Scout Finch. The story is narrated by Scout Finch, a young girl living in the American South.
2	B. Yossarian. The protagonist, Yossarian, faces absurd and contradictory situations in war.
3	B. The Jesus Prayer. Franny is obsessed with the Jesus Prayer as part of her spiritual quest.
4	C. To own a house.

QUESTIO N N.	CORRECT ANSWER
	The novel chronicles Mr. Biswas's quest to own his own house.
5	B. A girls' school in Edinburgh. Miss Brodie teaches at a girls' school in Edinburgh.
6	C. Leading a gang of delinquents. Alex is notorious for his violent behavior and leadership of a gang.
7	B. John Shade. The novel centers around a poem by John Shade, with an extensive commentary by Charles Kinbote.
8	A. Nurse Ratched. Nurse Ratched is the authoritarian figure in the psychiatric hospital.
9	B. Journalist. Esther Greenwood works as a guest editor for a magazine in New York City.
10	A. Ice-Nine. Ice-Nine is a pivotal element in the plot, with the ability to freeze water at room temperature.
11	D. A person or place known as "V." The novel involves the pursuit of something or someone known as "V."
12	B. Writes letters to famous people. Herzog writes unsent letters to friends, family, and famous figures.
13	B. Alec Leamas. The novel centers around Alec Leamas, a British spy during the Cold War.
14	B. Arrakis. The planet Arrakis, also known as Dune, is the central setting of the novel.
15	C. The Clutter family murders. The book is a detailed account of the murder of

QUESTIO N N.	CORRECT ANSWER
	the Clutter family in 1959.
16	C. The existence of an underground postal system. Oedipa investigates a mysterious symbol and a possible secret postal system.
17	B. Antoinette Cosway. The novel is a prequel to "Jane Eyre," focusing on the life of Antoinette Cosway, who becomes Bertha Mason.
18	A. The Buendía family. The novel tells the story of the Buendía family over several generations.
19	B. The devil and his retinue. The novel features a visit by the devil and his companions to Soviet Moscow.
20	C. A bounty hunter. Deckard is a bounty hunter tasked with "retiring" rogue androids.
21	C. Silkscreen printing. Warhol used silkscreen printing to create the "Marilyn Diptych."
22	C. Comic book panels. "Whaam!" was inspired by comic book panels, typical of Lichtenstein's pop art style.
23	C. Large blocks of color. Rothko's work is characterized by large, soft-edged blocks of color.
24	B. Drip painting. "Convergence" is a famous example of Pollock's drip painting technique.
25	B. 32. Warhol created 32 variations of the Campbell's Soup Cans.
26	D. Layering of three canvases. "Three Flags" features three overlaid canvases

QUESTIO N N.	CORRECT ANSWER
	of the American flag.
27	B. The sail-like shells. The Opera House is renowned for its unique sail-like design.
28	C. Urban housing. "Habitat 67" was designed as a pioneering model for urban housing.
29	C. Its futuristic design and curved forms. The TWA Flight Center is famous for its modern and futuristic design.
30	Correct: B. Seattle's Volunteer Park. "Black Sun" is a monumental sculpture located in Seattle's Volunteer Park.

e.   CARTOONS & COMICS 20 trivia

QUESTIO N N.	CORRECT ANSWER
1	A. Wilma. Wilma is Fred Flintstone's wife in "The Flintstones."
2	A. Astro. The family dog in "The Jetsons" is named Astro.
3	D. Hadji. Hadji is Jonny Quest's best friend in the series.
4	D. The Mystery Machine. The van is famously known as The Mystery Machine.
5	C. Clark Kent. Superman's alter ego is Clark Kent.
6	B. Gwen Stacy.

QUESTIO N N.	CORRECT ANSWER
	Gwen Stacy was one of Spider-Man's early love interests.
7	C. Professor X. Professor Charles Xavier, also known as Professor X, is the founder and leader of the X-Men.
8	B. Thor. Thor is one of the original founding members of the Avengers.
9	C. Mr. Fantastic. Mr. Fantastic, also known as Reed Richards, is the leader who can stretch his body.
10	B. Hal Jordan. Hal Jordan is the real name of the Silver Age Green Lantern
11	A. Officer Dibble. Officer Dibble is the beat cop constantly at odds with Top Cat.
12	C. Pet store. Magilla is perpetually for sale in a pet store.
13	B. Super strength and speed. Atom Ant possesses incredible strength and speed.
14	A. Morocco Mole. Morocco Mole assists Secret Squirrel in his missions.
15	A. Jan and Jace. Jan and Jace are Space Ghost's sidekicks.
16	A. Robin. Robin is Batman's loyal sidekick in the series.
17	A. A magic hat. Frosty comes to life when a magic hat is placed on his head.
18	C. Causing mischief. The Pink Panther is known for his mischievous

QUESTIO N N.	CORRECT ANSWER
	and humorous antics.
19	B. To catch a pigeon. They are constantly trying to catch a carrier pigeon.
20	B. Anger and stress. Bruce Banner transforms into the Hulk when he is angry or stressed.

f. SCIENCE 10 trivia

QUESTIO N N.	CORRECT ANSWER
1	C. Murray Gell-Mann and George Zweig. They independently proposed the quark model for fundamental particles.
2	E. Ruby laser. Theodore Maiman created the first working laser using a ruby crystal.
3	C. Yuri Gagarin. The Russian cosmonaut was the first human in space.
4	C. Arno Penzias and Robert Wilson. Their discovery supported the Big Bang theory.
5	C. Christiaan Barnard. He performed the first successful heart transplant.
6	B. Mariner 4. It provided the first close-up images of Mars.
7	A. Jocelyn Bell Burnell and Antony Hewish. They discovered pulsars in 1967.
8	B. Jack Kilby and Robert Noyce. They are credited with the independent

QUESTIO N N.	CORRECT ANSWER
	invention of the integrated circuit.
9	B. Anxiety. Valium, or diazepam, was widely prescribed for anxiety.
10	B. Computed Tomography (CT. scan) The development of the CT scan in the late 1960s revolutionized medical imaging by providing detailed cross-sectional views of the body.

g.   MUSIC 25rivia

QUESTIO N N.	CORRECT ANSWER
1	A. Bob Dylan. This song is often cited as one of the greatest songs in the history of popular music.
2	A. The Beatles. This song was a best-selling single and marked their breakthrough in the American market.
3	A. Aretha Franklin. Her version of the song became a landmark recording in 1967.
4	B. The Rolling Stones. This song is one of their most recognizable and enduring hits.
5	A. The Beach Boys. The song is celebrated for its complex sound and was a major hit.
6	A. The Beatles. "Hey Jude" is one of the band's most famous and beloved songs.

QUESTION N.	CORRECT ANSWER
7	A. The Doors. The song is one of their most popular and helped establish them as a leading band of the era.
8	A. The Temptations. "My Girl" is one of their most iconic and enduring songs.
9	A. Sam Cooke. The song is an anthem of the Civil Rights Movement.
10	A. Jimi Hendrix. "Purple Haze" is one of Hendrix's most famous and influential songs.
11	C. "A Day in the Life." The song is known for its innovative structure and the famous final chord.
12	B. Marvin Gaye. This version became one of his most famous songs.
13	A. Ben E. King. "Stand by Me" is a classic soul anthem.
14	A. Jimi Hendrix. While originally written by Bob Dylan, Hendrix's version is very wellknown.
15	A. The Mamas & the Papas. The song is one of their most enduring hits.
16	B. "Sympathy for the Devil." The song is notable for its distinctive rhythm and controversial lyrics.
17	A. Marvin Gaye. The song is a reflection on various societal issues of the time.
18	A. David Bowie. The song was released in conjunction with the Apollo 11 moon landing.

QUESTION N.	CORRECT ANSWER
19	A. Traditional folk song. The Animals' version became a huge hit.
20	A. Cream. The song is one of the band's most famous tracks.
21	B. Jimi Hendrix. Jimi Hendrix, an iconic guitarist, founded the rock band The Jimi Hendrix Experience in 1966. The band was known for its innovative sound and Hendrix's extraordinary guitar skills.
22	B. Peter, Paul, and Mary. Peter, Paul, and Mary were a folk music trio who gained fame in the 1960s. Their hit "Leaving on a Jet Plane," written by John Denver, became one of their most famous songs.
23	C. The Mothers of Invention (Frank Zappa). The Mothers of Invention, led by Frank Zappa, released "Freak Out!" in 1966. It is considered one of the first concept albums, blending rock, doo-wop, and experimental soundscapes.
24	A. The Fillmore. The Fillmore in San Francisco became a key venue for the 1960s counterculture and music scene. It hosted many famous artists and was central to the development of the "San Francisco Sound."
25	C. Jefferson Airplane. Jefferson Airplane, a pioneer of psychedelic rock, released "White Rabbit" in 1967. The song, with its Alice in Wonderland references, became a counterculture anthem.

CRUCIPUZZLE N. 1

```
D B G B L U F O N D A C W
E E U E B B O N A N Z A H
C R N A E I Z L U L S B A
E L S V N A Z L C O M O T
M E M E N L I Z M L H A S
B N O R Y S E A O D A D M
E S K A E A N D Y R R G Y
R E E D L C A E S A R R L
B R W E L L E S D G I O I
R L A S S I E E S N E U N
I I U I B U R N S E T C E
D N A C B E N N E T T H R
E G N A Y A R T H U R O Z
```

Hidden Words: Lucille Ball and Desi Arnaz.

CRUCIPUZZLE N. 2

```
B E N H U R G I A N T H D
G O D Z I L L A G E G N A
W N G T A Y L O R I A H V
I C H A P L I N E M L I I
L O D T R E L L W O L T S
D O E E M T C E S N A C E
E P R N A S N K K R B H C
R E K E E N W P A O O C L
R R E L B A E F Z E U O I
E R L B H E G R A N T C F
L E L G A R L A N D E K T
W A Y N E O G I G I V N D
S U N S E T B L V D E E S
```

Hidden Words: Gentlemen Prefer Blondes

CRUCIPUZZLE N. 3

Hidden Words: Mickey Mantle and Yogi Berra

CRUCIPUZZLE N. 4

Hidden Words: Ernest Hemingway

CRUCIPUZZLE N. 5

```
T T R H T A R Z A N E A O
W D O N A L D D U C K T N
E D A I R O N M A N U A D
E V D P O P E Y E L M A C
E T R N C T U R P K E B I
Y A U B A E S O W H G L N
F R N E S T D A G W O O D
P C N T P I H U S A O N E
D H E T E N J D N Y F D R
T I R Y R T H E O T Y I E
V E R O N I C A O H P E L
B A T M A N E L P O I C L
P E T E R P A N Y R A N A
```

Hidden Words: The Adventures of Paddy the Pelican

CRUCIPUZZLE N. 6

```
C U R I E Y U K A W A T W
H R P L A N C K Y D E O O
A F I B A R D E E N M W X
N E W C Y B K R R A I N W
D R I B K A L O G O S E I
R M G S E A B O R G I S E
A I N L B U S H C B E L N
S T E L L E R N A H Y U E
E C R U T H E R F O R D R
K S H A N N O N H L E H I
H A H N C L I B B Y O A C
A L V A R E Z H U B B L E
R K I W A L D D B E T H E
```

Hidden Words: Deoxyribose Nucleic Acid

CRUCIPUZZLE N. 7

Hidden Words: The Battle of New Orleans

CRUCIPUZZLE N. 8

Hidden Words: The Andy Griffith Show

CRUCIPUZZLE N. 9

Hidden Words: The Manchurian Candidate

CRUCIPUZZLE N. 10

Hidden Words: Wilton Norman Chamberlain

CRUCIPUZZLE N. 11

Hidden Words: I Know Why the Caged Bird Sings

CRUCIPUZZLE N. 12

```
M B A M M B A M M X S I A
C A R N O L D H I W C R T
G T R A R J T L L I O O O
E M I V E N E W B L O N P
R A R O I F V T E E B M C
A N W T O N L I S E Y A A
L S N O O P Y U S O T N T
D I G S M U R F C I N Y R
T A N T M A N N L Y O O C
M A Q U A M A N H A H N M
R I C A S P E R S T S O T
B U L L W I N K L E T H M
W O N D E R W O M A N A S
```

Hidden Words: A Charlie Brown Christmas (1965.

CRUCIPUZZLE N. 13

```
C H A N D R A S E K H A R
T E L L E R U L A N D S R
I C H A V W D B B E T H E
Y U K A W A I R I D G O I
D Y S O N T R P H N E C N
F E R M I S A E S A L K S
C I A L L O C W Z I L L T
G R B O R N W P I S M E E
L F I E B O H M Y G A Y I
A N M C M P A U L I N G N
S L E A K E Y T O W N E S
E A G N S C H W I N G E R
R T O M O N A G A B O H R
```

Hidden Words: Richard Phillips Feynman

CRUCIPUZZLE N. 14

```
C P M C L E A N C T C C R
A A A H N S U P R E M E S
S T R A E S C H E R N E K
H S L E D G E B A O E O I
O Y E C O O K E M T L S N
D A Y R E D D I N G S R K
O E F O U R S E A S O N S
O R B I S O N S T O N E S
R M A D Z E P P E L I N G
S D R E F R A N K L I N E
E Y A R D B I R D S I Y F
B B U F F A L O O K A R W
A L B E A T L E S G K I N
```

Hidden Words: These Boots Are Made for Walkin'

☀ HERE IS YOU FREE GIFT!

👆 SCAN HERE TO DOWNLOAD IT

300 FLASHCARDS WITH ALL THE QUESTIONS AND ANSWERS